Understanding
The Holy Spirit

by James Hankins

ISBN: 979-8-9986881-0-2

www.jameshankinsministries.org

CONTENTS

Our Prayer Together

Father I come to you In the name of Jesus, and I ask you to set me on fire with your Holy Spirit. You're all I want and nothing else! I yield my heart to your loving fire, and I ask you to consume me completely my Lord. Reveal your heart to me because I really want to know you deeply.

Lord, I know you long for me with a jealous love, may I never yield my precious life to Idols, temptations, or the fleeting desires of this world. Instead, let my heart be a sacred altar, purified and set ablaze by your presence. Make me a living flame, burning with passion for you alone, shining as a beacon of your glory, and consumed by the fire of your love.

Lord, I know that the fire of your presence falls upon surrendered lives. So I come before you in humility, laying down my pride, and all I cling to. As I bow In reverence, I offer myself wholly to you, as a living sacrifice upon your altar. Let your consuming fire purify me, refine me, and set me ablaze, until nothing remains but a heart fully yielded to you.

May the leading of your Holy Spirit guide me into all truth and transform me as I seek you with all of my heart. I love you so much Jesus. Thank you for giving me new life and giving me the best gift, your Holy Spirit. In Jesus name I pray, Amen.

For the Lord your God Is a consuming fire, a jealous God.
Deuteronomy 4:24 NKJV

CHAPTER 1

Jesus Introduces the Holy Spirit

*And I will ask the Father, and **He will give you another Helper** (Comforter, Advocate, Intercessor — Counselor, Strengthener, Standby), to be with you forever — the **Spirit of Truth**, whom the world cannot receive [and take to its heart] because it does not see Him or know Him, but you know Him because He (**the Holy Spirit**) remains with you continually and will be **IN** you. -John 14:16-17 AMP*

Picture yourself 2000 years ago as one of the disciples following Jesus. Put yourself in their shoes. Pretend you can see what they see and feel what they feel and know what they know.

Imagine listening to Jesus teach about the kingdom of God, watching him heal people and deliver them from demons, seeing him forgive people like the adulterous woman. Visualize the man with leprosy as he came to Jesus (Matthew 8), kneeling and saying, "Lord, if you are willing, you can heal me and make me clean." Picture Jesus putting His hand on his shoulder and looking at him with eyes full of compassion, saying to him, "Yes, I am willing. Be healed." How would you feel as you watched that man cry because he was experiencing a new kind of love, a miracle from God Himself?

Can you imagine the love and personal value Jesus gave to the disciples?

When Jesus looked at His disciples, they could probably sense that He knew everything about them, yet loved them with a love that goes beyond human understanding — a love that only can come from God Himself.

This radical love caused the disciples to follow Jesus even though it would eventually cost them their lives. Their love for Jesus grew and grew because they shared life with Him. They stayed where He stayed, they ate what He ate, they walked with Him everyday, they talked with Him everyday! They knew and understood Him like family because they spent all their time with Him. They laughed with Jesus, and I'm sure He was the most joyful man they had ever known. His very presence cast out fears, and they found complete peace in Him, because He is God. We know that where there is perfect love, there is no fear. Each disciple probably felt fully seen, heard, and valued while with Jesus. They had never experienced that before. They were fully loved by their Creator, and for the first time since the Garden, they were able to feel a part of that love. As His followers they were **completely dependent on Him** for everything.

Now, Jesus knew that His time on earth was short, so He began to talk to His disciples about things to come and their future together. He began to introduce the Holy Spirit, who would continue to be with them just as He had.

You have to understand that the disciples had no concept of what receiving the Holy Spirit looked like.

So, Jesus had to teach them about the Holy Spirit. Naturally, after experiencing such deep companionship with Him, they would likely feel abandoned and afraid as Jesus talked about His death, burial, resurrection, and ascension to the Father.

This explains why Jesus makes these statements:

John 14:27
"Let not your heart be troubled, neither let it be afraid. You have heard Me say to you, 'I am going away and coming back to you.'"

John 14:16
"I will not leave you orphans (I will not abandon you)"

Here are a few scriptures of Jesus slowly introducing the person of the Holy Spirit:

Jesus speaking In John 14:16-24

And I will pray the Father, and He will give you another Helper, that He may abide with you forever — the Spirit of truth, whom the world cannot receive, because it neither sees Him nor knows Him; but you know Him, for He dwells with you and will be in you.

*I will **not leave you orphans**; I will come to you. A little while longer and the world will see Me no more, but you will see Me. Because I live, you will live also. At that day you will know that I am in My Father, and you in Me, and **I in you**.*

He who has My commandments and keeps them, it is he who loves Me. And he who loves Me will be loved by My Father, and **I will love him and manifest Myself to him.**

Jesus answered and said to him, "If anyone loves Me, he will keep My word; and My Father will love him, and **We will come to him and make Our home with him**.

Jesus manifests Himself to us by the Holy Spirit

Jesus speaking in John 14:25-29

These things I have spoken to you while being present with you. But the Helper, the **Holy Spirit**, whom the Father will send in My name, **He will teach you all things, and bring to your remembrance all things that I said to you.** Peace I leave with you, My peace I give to you; not as the world gives do I give to you.

Let not your heart be troubled, neither let it be afraid. You have heard Me say to you, '**I am going away and coming back to you.**' If you loved Me, you would rejoice because I said, 'I am going to the Father,' for My Father is greater than I. And now I have told you before it comes, that when it does come to pass, you may believe.

Jesus speaking In John 16:13-15

However, when He, the **Spirit of truth**, has come, **He will guide you** into all truth; for He will not speak on

*His own authority, but **whatever He hears He will speak**; and **He will tell you things to come.***

He will glorify Me, for He will take of what is Mine and declare it to you.

*All things that the Father has are Mine. Therefore I said that **He will take of Mine and declare it to you.***

Notice, Jesus was trying to prepare their hearts to know and understand they wouldn't be left alone, because another would come after Him and continue to reveal the kingdom of God to them and empower them to continue preaching the message of Jesus.

But don't miss this: Jesus said, "IT IS BETTER that I go away, or else the HELPER will not come."

How extraordinary must life with the Holy Spirit be, to surpass the experience of walking physically with Jesus each day?

John 16:7 NKJV
*Nevertheless I tell you the truth. It is to **your advantage that I go away**; for if I do not go away, **the Helper will not come** to you; but **if I depart, I will send Him (the Holy Spirit) to you**.*

Jesus is also known as Emmanuel, which means "God with us." He walked **with** the disciples. But Jesus knew something greater needed to take place. He needed to be able to walk with everyone who wanted to receive Him.

He was preparing to make His home **IN US**. This represents a profound love that God has for us; Jesus desired not only to be with us but also to dwell within us.

Let's look at John 14:22-23 again:

> *Judas (not Iscariot) said to Him, "Lord, **how is it that You will manifest Yourself to us**, and not to the world?" Jesus answered and said to him, "If anyone loves Me, he will keep My word; and My Father will love him, and **We will come to him and make our home with him.***

What a marvelous thing that God would choose us to be His dwelling place.

> *1 Corinthians 6:19 AMPC*
> *Do you not know that your body is the temple (the very sanctuary) of **the Holy Spirit Who lives within you**, Whom you have received [as a Gift] from God? You are not your own.*

Lets look at what scripture tells us in John 7:37-39:

> *On the last day, that great day of the feast, Jesus stood and cried out, saying, "If anyone thirsts, let him come to Me and drink. He who believes in Me, as the Scripture has said, out of his heart will flow rivers of living water."*

> *But this He spoke concerning **the Spirit**, whom those believing in Him would receive; for **the Holy Spirit***

was not yet given, because Jesus was not yet glorified.

Well, Jesus is **NOW glorified**. His crucifixion, death, and resurrection has already taken place.

So let's read Acts 1:1-5, 8-9 to see what happens now:

The first account I made, Theophilus, was about all the things that Jesus began to do and to teach until the day when He ascended to heaven, after He had by the Holy Spirit given instruction to the apostles whom He had chosen.

To these [men] He also showed Himself alive after His suffering, by many infallible proofs and unquestionable demonstrations, appearing to them over a period of forty days and talking to them about the things concerning the kingdom of God.

*While being together and eating with them, He commanded them **not to leave Jerusalem, but to wait for what the Father had promised,** "Of which," He said, "you have heard Me speak. For John baptized with water, but you will be **baptized and empowered with the Holy Spirit**, not long from now."*

***But you will receive power and ability when the Holy Spirit comes upon you;** and you will be My witnesses [to tell people about Me] both in Jerusalem and in all Judea, and Samaria, and even to the ends of the earth."*

And after He said these things, He was caught up as they looked on, and a cloud took Him up out of their sight.

Now keep imagining you are with the disciples in this moment. Do you remember what Jesus instructed them to do?

Remember, Jesus was not with them, and they were stressed and probably bewildered after watching Jesus ascend and leave them. In this moment, they were clinging to the last thing Jesus told them, which was, "**DO NOT LEAVE** Jerusalem, but **WAIT** for what the Father had promised." They were waiting for the Father's promise of the **HOLY SPIRIT!**

The drama unfolds in Acts 2. Keep in mind, the disciples had no idea what receiving the Holy Spirit would look like. They had never seen anyone filled with the Holy Spirit before. This was **completely new** to all of them. So they went to the upper room to wait for the Holy Spirit and fellowshipped together, knowing this was what Jesus told them to do. And together, they waited.

Acts 2:1-4 NKJV

When the Day of Pentecost had fully come, they were all in one accord in one place. And suddenly there came a sound from heaven, as of a rushing mighty wind, and it filled the whole house where they were sitting. Then there appeared to them divided tongues, as of fire, and one sat upon each of them.

*And they were all filled with the Holy Spirit and
began to speak with other tongues, as the Spirit gave
them utterance*

What an introduction to the Holy Spirit! This is the One Jesus was teaching them about, the Helper they would receive!

*John 14:16-17 AMP
And I will ask the Father, and **He will give you
another Helper** (Comforter, Advocate, Intercessor —
Counselor, Strengthener, Standby), to be with you
forever — the **Spirit of Truth**, whom the world cannot
receive [and take to its heart] because it does not see
Him or know Him, but you know Him because He (**the
Holy Spirit**) remains with you continually and will be
IN you.*

**Experience the fullness of Jesus through the baptism of
the Holy Spirit.**

The disciples have now stepped Into a WHOLE NEW form of communication with God. They now have to depend completely on the Holy Spirit.

Remember, this is all new to them. This is a dramatic transition for them. They went from **following Jesus,** whom they could **see with their eyes** and **hear with their ears**, to now receiving the Holy Spirit, whom **they could not see. This completely changes** how they walk with God. God has now moved into their own spirits. They must now learn how to listen on the inside instead of the outside.

Their new form of communication with God is now prayer and communion with the Holy Spirit, and He is accessible all the time. The disciples had walked with Jesus (as a man), but now they began to walk with the Holy Spirit dwelling in them. This marks the moment when Jesus' disciples transformed into the New Testament Church, a community of believers empowered by and guided by the Holy Spirit.

This means we are now under the inspiration, leadership, and guidance of the Holy Spirit, and we must depend on the Holy Spirit to instruct and help us, just as the disciples did.

This word "*depend*" is a verb, and it means to be controlled or determined by. It can also mean to rely upon, trust in, lean on, and support oneself.

Our journey as disciples of Jesus reaches its greatest purpose and power when we surrender every part of our being to the gentle and transformational leadership of the Holy Spirit.

Romans 8:14 NKJV
"For as many as are led by the Spirit of God, these are sons of God."

CHAPTER 2

The Role of the Holy Spirit

So what is the role of the Holy Spirit in our lives? The main and basic role of the Holy Spirit is to reveal Jesus to our hearts. Also, to reveal all that we have in Christ as an inheritance and to lead us Into the purpose that God has for us.

Some of the Key roles of the Holy Spirit in our lives include:

- Guidance and Wisdom - He leads us Into truth and helps us understand God's will (John 16:13)

- Transformation/Sanctification - He sanctifies us, making us more like Jesus. (2 Corinthians 3:18)

- Deep hunger for The Word of God (John 16:13-15)

- Manifest Gods tangible presence to us and through us (John 14:21, Acts 4:18-19)

- Reveal the love of God to our hearts (Romans 5:5)

- Spiritual Gifts - The Holy Spirit gives us gifts to build up the church (1 Corinthians 12:4-11)

- Boldness and Power: The Holy Spirit empowers believers to witness and spread the Gospel (Acts 1:8).

- Growth into maturity as sons and daughters of God, by revealing the Son of God to us in such a way that we become "mature, lacking nothing, so we attain to the whole measure of the fullness of Christ."

- Growth in our understanding of the deep things of God, so that we may experience His love and power in a continual, transformative way (1 Corinthians 2:9-10).

We can see this in 1 Corinthians 2:9-10:

> But as it is written: "Eye has not seen, nor ear heard, nor have entered into the heart of man the things which God has prepared for those who love Him."

> But God has **revealed them to us through His Spirit**. For the Spirit searches all things, yes, the **deep things of God.**

> Romans 5.5 says, "Hope does not disappoint us because the **love of God has been poured into our hearts by the Holy Spirit.**"

So we see right there that the Holy Spirit is the one who reveals the love of God to our hearts, that we may know Him and fellowship with Jesus — initiating that intimate, deep, transformative relationship He paid at the cross for us to have.

My testimony of being filled with the Holy Spirit

I want to give you my testimony about my encounter with the Holy Spirit, being baptized with the Holy Spirit, and how the role of the Holy Spirit completely transformed my life. I grew up hearing about God, but I never saw anyone talking about the Holy Spirit or walking in the power of God.

I knew that there had to be more than just hearing a good message on Sunday and then being a "good person." That was just a waste of time to me. I wanted something real, transformative, and powerful!

In 2012, God heard my prayer. I was invited to church by one of my friends, and when I got to the church I needed to go to the bathroom. While I was washing my hands, a guy I didn't know approached me and said my name. He said, "Hey, James?" I said, "Yes? How do you know my name? I don't know you." He laughed and said, "I know you don't know me, let's talk outside the bathroom." As we walked into the lobby of the church, he explained to me that God had spoken to him that morning and told him that he would meet a blonde guy named James, and to "ask him what he desires."

When I heard how he supernaturally knew my name, I was amazed at how close his relationship with God was. I wanted that too! It was what I was searching for! When he asked me what I desired, I told him I wanted to understand about speaking in tongues. He told me to meet him after the service. Now, this service was unlike anything I have experienced. I began to cry and feel the tangible presence of God. After the service ended, I met with the guy from the bathroom. He explained to me that he was the youth pastor of that church. Then he invited me to go into the main sanctuary and sit in the front to talk with him.

I began to ask him questions about speaking in tongues. He told me this was a gift that comes when you are baptized in the Holy Spirit. At this point I had no idea what being "baptized in the Holy Spirit" was, but I didn't care!

I wanted all that God had for me! I was so hungry for the deep things of God.

He then told me, "If you want this, then ask God for it!" Immediately, I threw up my hands and said, " God, I ask you to ...." Before I even could ask God for the Holy Spirit, the power of God surged through me. My whole body began to shake, and I began to speak in tongues! What I experienced could never be truly expressed in words. I began to cry for a couple of minutes; then I began to laugh with the deepest joy I have ever known. I felt the most pure, holy, and powerful love flood my entire body.

I spoke in tongues for a long time nonstop because the power of God was so strong all over me. It was so strong I could not even stand up. Then all of the sudden I started to feel something in my spirit begin to bubble up out of me, and I began to prophesy. This was the first time the Holy Spirit began to prophesy through me. He said, "I am coming soon! I am coming soon! I am coming for my church!"

I knew this was exactly what I had been searching for my whole life. This was REAL. This was powerful. The longing of my heart was satisfied. It was the Holy Spirit flooding me with the fullness of God. I went from knowing God to being FULL of GOD.

Keep in mind I did not know what was happening. The youth pastor asked me if I understood what I said. I told him I did not. He began to explain to me about the book of Revelation and the second coming of Jesus. It was very hard to hold a conversation because I couldn't stop speaking in tongues and my body kept shaking. In fact, for three days afterwards, my body continually shook with the power of God.

When I got home, I locked myself in my room to pray and read the Bible for hours until I fell asleep. I wanted to know EVERYTHING about the Holy Spirit. My whole life was consumed with God. All I wanted was Him. I wanted EVERYTHING God had for me. My heart ached to know Him so deeply.

He captivated my heart in such a way that all I wanted to do was be with Him and seek His face, and to know His Love and Power. He captivated my heart in such a way that all I wanted to do was be with Him and seek His face, and to know His Love and Power.

I suddenly had a strong appetite for the Bible. I would read everything! I became so passionate for God that I would literally just get the highlighter and highlight the entire page. I didn't even underline scriptures. I understood what David meant when he wrote in Psalms,

"My whole body yearns and longs for you, my soul thirsts for you."

I encountered the scripture in Matthew 10:8 that says, "Heal the sick, raise the dead, cleanse the lepers, cast out demons. Freely you have received, freely give. "

I immediately took that scripture to heart and applied it. I thought to myself, "Where are some sick people?" I went to the nearest grocery store and looked for anyone who was hurting.

I found this lady who was walking with a limp. I asked her, "Can I pray for you?" She said yes like she thought I would go home and add her to my prayer list. But I was full of the Holy Spirit and I believed for miracles NOW! I told the lady, "I believe Jesus will heal you now! Can I pray for you now?" She agreed.

So I laid hands on her and spoke to her pain and said, "Be healed in the name of Jesus!" Immediately she started to cry, and I asked, "What is happening? " She told me she felt fire on her back, and all the pain was gone. She told me she had been suffering this horrible pain for 12 years. I also read in the Bible about the gifts of the Holy Spirit, and I noticed that 1 Corinthians 14:1 says, "Pursue love, and desire spiritual gifts, but especially that you may prophesy." I didn't know there were gifts of the Holy Spirit, so I asked God for these as the scripture said.

After this, I was walking in the mall, and as I passed someone, I heard the Holy Spirit tell me this person had an eye problem in his left eye. I turned around and ran towards him, stopped him and said, "I know this may be random, but do you have any problems with your left eye?" He said, "Yes, I do! I went in for surgery a few years ago, and they made a mistake on my eye, and now I am 80% blind in this eye."

I told him, "God told me you had this problem. That's why I stopped you. I believe Jesus can heal you. Will you let me pray for you?" He said yes. So I said, "In the name of Jesus, I command your eye to open now and be healed." In that very moment, this person got completely healed in his left eye. This was just the beginning of walking with the Holy Spirit! There is an abundance to learn and experience with God. He is endlessly captivating, consistently leaving me in awe of His presence.

Power of God Falls on Young people

I began to tell everyone about the Holy Spirit. I would have people come to my house specifically to get filled with the Holy Spirit. I would get calls late at night from old friends and new, and they would come hungering for the Holy Spirit.

The power of God would fall on these young guys in such an unusual and powerful way. I remember praying for this one guy who was much larger than me. I told him to lift his hands and ask Jesus to fill him with the Holy Spirit. When he lifted his hand, I said, "Be filled with the Holy Spirit and fire!" I felt electricity flow out of me, and immediately this huge guy was lifted off the ground and thrown back five feet by the power of God. He began to speak in tongues and received a vision from Jesus.

After these guys got filled with the Holy Spirit, they left my house and went to get in their car. But they were so touched by the power of God that they could not stand. They had to have their friends drive their car.

This was role of the Holy Spirit in my life: making the Word of God come alive, revealing the deep things of God to me, impacting people's lives, healing people, delivering people, and giving people the freedom Jesus paid for on the Cross. You see, the Holy Spirit doesn't come upon you and fill you with power so you sit on your hands.

He's going to fill you with power, which is the ability to do things that need to get done. When Jesus's disciples were baptized in the Holy Spirit, they began to preach the gospel under the inspiration of the Spirit of God. Miracles were performed. People would get healed, delivered, and set free by the power of the Holy Spirit.

In Luke 4:18, we can see what happens when the Holy Spirit fulfills His role. Jesus reads from Isaiah, "The Spirit of the Lord is upon me, because He has anointed me to preach the gospel to the poor. He has sent me to heal the brokenhearted, to proclaim liberty to the captives and recovery of sight to the blind, to set at liberty those who are oppressed."

The same Spirit who was active in the old prophets came to us through Jesus so that *all* who follow Him could have access to these ministries.

Watch how the apostle Paul speaks about his ministry:

1 Corinthians 2:4- "And my speech and my preaching were not with persuasive words of human wisdom, but in demonstration of the Spirit and of power."

1 Thessalonians 1:5 — "Because our gospel came to you not only in word, but also in power, in the Holy Spirit, and with great conviction — just as you know we lived among you for your sake."

1 Corinthians 4:20- "For the kingdom of God is not a matter of talk but of power."

In my own ministry, I wanted people to be healed and set free. The passion that was in Jesus was the passion that was in me because the same Spirit that came upon Jesus in the Jordan River, and upon all the apostles in Acts 2, came upon me with the same result: people got healed, set free, Jesus was preached, and my life began to be completely transformed by the power of the Holy Spirit.

The Holy Spirit opened my eyes. I began to operate in the gifts of the Holy Spirit. I began to see things in the Spirit. I began to have spiritual dreams. I began to have visions. I began to prophesy. I began to see demons manifest. I began to see all these supernatural things that I had previously never seen. But the most transformative thing that happened to me was that I desperately desired to know God. My hunger for the Word of God was so intense, and I wanted to know everything about Him. Holy Spirit began to give me understanding of all the

the promises that were in the Bible. I began to have supernatural wisdom and revelation when I read the scriptures.

His role in my life was very profound, opening the love of Jesus to my heart, and transforming me into His image.

The Holy Spirit will reveal the Word of God to you, that you may grow up in Him, built up and edified by the Word of God, that you may know all the promises of God, know all that God is.

The Bible says that people perish for a lack of knowledge (Hosea 4:6). It is imperative that the Holy Spirit reveals the Word of God to us so we can be transformed.

Ephesians 1:1 says,
"May He give you the spirit of wisdom and revelation
so that you may know Him better."

We see right there that the Holy Spirit is the one who reveals God by giving us wisdom and revelation about who He is.

The Holy Spirit's job is not only to give us gifts that can help other people (although that in itself is a wonderful blessing), but to **reveal Jesus** and **His love to our hearts,** so we can be **changed and transformed.**

CHAPTER 3

The Promise of the Holy Spirit

Did you know that Jesus promises to fill us with the Holy Spirit? What a precious *promise* of the Father. What a precious honor to be able to be a dwelling place of His Spirit.

God Anointed Leaders in the Old Testament with the Holy Spirit

In the Old Testament, the Holy Spirit would only come upon each minister or each king to do a particular service for the Lord. Then, when that assignment was completed, the Holy Spirit would go to the next king or prophet at a certain time. Now, Jesus promises us the Holy Spirit to come dwell *in* us.

Jesus talks about the Holy Spirit in John 7:37.

> *On the last day, the great day of the feast, Jesus stood and cried out saying, "If anyone thirsts, let him come to me and drink. For he who believes in me, as the scripture has said, out of his heart will flow rivers of living water."*

But this he spoke concerning the Spirit, whom those believing in him would receive. For the Holy Spirit was not yet given, because Jesus was not yet glorified.

The reason why the Holy Spirit was not yet given is because Jesus had not yet been glorified. In the Old Testament, God dwelt in the Ark of the Covenant, which was in the Holy of Holies. No man could enter because it was so holy; if any man did dare enter, he would die instantly. That's because there cannot be any sin in the presence of God. A sinless, righteous temple is the only place that the Spirit of God Himself can dwell.

Our Body is the Sanctuary of God's Spirit

If the Holy Spirit entered us before we were made holy, we would die, too. But because Jesus took on our sins at the cross, we are able to take on the righteousness of God, regardless of our past, present, and future sins. The exchange was complete. Through the sacrifice of our sinless Lamb, Jesus, we are made holy once and for all. We are made clean, whole, and righteous, and that makes us a perfect dwelling place for the Holy Spirit of God.

Here are several scriptures that demonstrate how your body serves as the sacred home for God's spirit.

Romans 8:9 NKJV
*But you are not in the flesh but in the Spirit, if indeed the **Spirit of God dwells in you**. Now if anyone does not have the Spirit of Christ, he is not His.*

Acts 17:24 NKJV
God, who made the world and everything in it, since
*He is Lord of heaven and earth, **does not dwell in***
temples made with hands.

1 Corinthians 6:19 NKJV
*Or do you not know that **your body** is the **temple of***
***the Holy Spirit** who is in you, whom you have from*
God, and you are not your own?

Now let's look at another Scripture where Jesus promises the Holy Spirit.

John 14:15-17
If you love me, keep my commandments. And I will
pray to the Father, and He will give you another
Helper, that He may abide with you forever.

The Spirit of truth whom the world cannot receive,
because it neither sees Him nor knows Him. But you
know Him, for He dwells with you and will be in you. I
will not leave you orphans, I will come to you.

"Holy Spirit" here is the Greek word *parakletos*, which means "one called alongside to help." The Holy Spirit is the Spirit of Jesus. Jesus says, "for He dwells with you and will be in you." "Will be" is future tense. Jesus is Emmanuel, God with us. Here He is telling the disciples that He will come to them Himself, but He will lead them inwardly rather than outwardly.

Let's turn our attention to *Acts 2:1-18* to see what

happened to the disciples after the Holy Spirit had been poured out.

When the Day of Pentecost had fully come, they were all with one accord in one place. And suddenly there came a sound from heaven, as of a rushing mighty wind, and it filled the whole house where they were sitting. Then there appeared to them divided tongues, as of fire, and one sat upon each of them. And they were all filled with the Holy Spirit and began to speak with other tongues, as the Spirit gave them utterance.

The Crowd's Response

And there were dwelling in Jerusalem Jews, devout men, from every nation under heaven. And when this sound occurred, the multitude came together, and were confused, because everyone heard them speak in his own language.

Then they were all amazed and marveled, saying to one another, "Look, are not all these who speak Galileans? And how is it that we hear, each in our own language in which we were born?

we hear them speaking in our own tongues the wonderful works of God." So they were all amazed and perplexed, saying to one another, "Whatever could this mean?" Others mocking said, "They are drunk with wine."

Peter's message to the people

But Peter, standing up with the eleven, raised his voice and said to them, "Men of Judea and all who dwell in Jerusalem, let this be known to you, and heed my words. For these are not drunk, as you suppose, since it is only the third hour of the day.

But this is what was spoken by the prophet Joel: 'And it shall come to pass in the last days, says God, That I will pour out of My Spirit on all flesh; Your sons and your daughters shall prophesy, Your young men shall see visions, Your old men shall dream dreams. And on My menservants and on My maidservants I will pour out My Spirit in those days; And they shall prophesy.

So we see, the power of the Holy Spirit came and filled the whole place with a mighty rushing wind. Tongues of fire appeared over their heads, and they began to speak in tongues and prophesy, and then proclaim the message of Christ given in diverse languages. Many people thought they were drunk, because they were stumbling under the weight of the presence of God, but Peter gave a speech to tell them exactly what was happening.

*Acts 2:32–33 This Jesus God raised up, and of that we are all witnesses. Being therefore exalted at the right hand of God, and having received from the Father the promise of the Holy Spirit, he has poured out this that you yourselves are **seeing and hearing.***

I want you to also notice that it says they were "seeing and hearing." What were they seeing and hearing?

Acts 2:11-13
how is it that **we hear**, each **in our own language** in which we were born? We **hear** them speaking in our own tongues **the wonderful works of God**." So they were all amazed and perplexed, saying to one another, "Whatever could this mean?" Others mocking said, "They are drunk with wine."

Seeing

They where <u>seeing</u> the disciples under the power and influence of the Holy Spirit, mocking them saying they were drunk because they didn't understand what was happening.

Hearing

They were <u>hearing</u> the disciples praying in tongues. They were speaking the mysteries of God. This was one of the gifts of the Holy Spirit that had been poured out, something we receive when we are filled with the Holy Spirit. In this particular case, the gift of diversities of tongues mentioned in 1 Corinthians 12 was in operation, because we see the groups of people heard their native languages being spoken through the disciples by the Holy Spirit.

Personal Prayer Language in Tongues vs. The Gift of Diversity of Tongues from 1 Corinthians 12

When you receive the Holy Spirit and begin to speak in tongues, this particular tongues that you receive when you get filled the Holy Spirit is your personal prayer language.

This is different from the gift of Diverse Tongues, which is one of the nine gifts of the Holy Spirit mentioned in 1 Corinthians 12. Those special gifts operate as He wills when the Holy Spirit comes upon you to minister.

Here, we are focusing on the personal prayer language that you receive once filled with the Holy Spirit. Since this is your personal prayer language, you have the ability to choose when to pray in tongues at any time. This personal prayer language serves to edify yourself.

Jude 1:20 says, But you, beloved, building yourselves up on your most holy faith, praying in the Holy Spirit

(Speaking in tongues, is often referred to as praying in the spirit or praying with the spirit.) Let's also look at another scripture about speaking in tongues as your prayer language.

1 Corinthians 14:2,4 NKJV
Verse 2, For he who speaks in a tongue does not speak to men but to God, for no one understands him; however, in the spirit he speaks mysteries.

Verse 4, He who speaks in a tongue edifies himself, but he who prophesies edifies the church.

I would also like to mention that not only can you pray in tongues, but you can also express your worship to God by singing in tongues.

1 Corinthians 14:15
What is it then? I will pray with the spirit, and I will pray with the understanding also: I will sing with the spirit, and I will sing with the understanding also

So now let's look at this next verse in Acts 2:38.

"Then Peter said to them, repent and let every one of you be baptized into the name of Jesus Christ for the remissions and forgiveness of sins."

The people obeyed, and at that point, they received salvation based on the finished work of the cross.

*Then Peter said, "**And you shall receive** the gift of the Holy Spirit," just as the others had already received the Holy Spirit.*

Notice it says '**and you shall receive**.' The definition of the word "and" means in conjunction with.

The term "conjunction" is defined as: the action or an instance of two or more events or things occurring at the same point in time or space.

Therefore, it's important for you to know that after they were baptized in the name of Jesus Christ for the remission and forgiveness of sins, they *also* received the baptism of the Holy Spirit, just like the disciples experienced in the upper room when they spoke in tongues.

Lets continue In this scripture highlighting the promise of the baptism of the Holy Spirit is for everyone that Is a follower of Jesus.

> Then Peter said, "**And you shall receive** the gift of the Holy Spirit," just as the others had already received the Holy Spirit. For **the promise is for you and to your children and to all who are far off**, to as many as the Lord God will call.

This verse shows that the gift of the Holy Spirit with speaking in other tongues, which comes with the gift of the Holy Spirit, is a gift for all. It's not just for certain "chosen" people, or just for the disciples back then because they were so anointed. No, it is for all believers.

> Romans 2:11 says, "For God does not show favoritism."

Isn't that such a beautiful thing that Jesus would give us the Holy Spirit to come dwell in us and fill us with power from on high to be able to fulfill His mission on this earth?

Let's jump to *Acts 19:1-6*, as it clearly illustrates the same concept.

> And it happened, while Apollos was at Corinth, that Paul, having passed through the upper regions, came to Ephesus. And finding some disciples he said to

them, **"Did you receive the Holy Spirit when you believed?"**

So they said to him, "We have not so much as heard whether there is a Holy Spirit." And he said to them, "Into what then were you baptized?" So they said, "Into John's baptism." Then Paul said, "John indeed baptized with a baptism of repentance, saying to the people that they should believe on Him who would come after him, that is, on Christ Jesus."

When they heard this, **they were baptized in the name of the Lord Jesus.** And when Paul had laid hands on them, the **Holy Spirit came upon them, and they spoke with tongues and prophesied.**

Now, there's one final point I'd like to discuss regarding the Holy Spirit being a promise for all.

God desires a close relationship with you through the Holy Spirit

In the Old Testament, the Holy Spirit would dwell with the Israelites and would come upon individuals at certain times to fulfill a purpose. But Jesus wanted to be in us and dwell in us and lead us from within. He gave us powerful evidence of His desire for this indwelling when He was crucified.

Matthew 27 tells us that, as Jesus died, the curtain in the temple was ripped "from top to bottom." This curtain was likely about 4 inches thick and 60 feet high. It separated the Holy of Holies, where the Spirit of God lived, from the areas where people were allowed to enter. Only the High Priest was allowed in the Holy of Holies, and only after he had been purified by sacrifices.

But as Jesus completed the ultimate sacrifice through His death, an earthquake occurred, the earth split in several places, and this curtain was ripped "from top to bottom." Man did not rip the curtain, because if that was the case, it would be ripped from bottom to top.

In the moment of Jesus's death, God came out from behind the curtain. The Holy Spirit came out of that place made by human hands to come dwell in us as a people.

Isn't that beautiful? It's wonderful, good news. Jesus wanted to dwell in us by the Holy Spirit so he could lead us inwardly because we are His disciples. He told us that the Holy Spirit would teach us. He would help us. He would guide us. He would counsel us. He would give us wisdom and strength. And He would remind us of everything that Jesus spoke.

God desires to have fellowship with you by His Holy Spirit living in you. That is how He achieves that fellowship. The next time you pray, I want you to be very aware that you are the temple of the Holy Spirit, and I want you to be in reverence of the presence of God. You are the dwelling place of God's Spirit because you have received the promise of the Father.

CHAPTER 4

The Power of the Holy Spirit

What is the power of the Holy Spirit? That word "power" means the *ability* to do things. The Holy Spirit's power simply represents His *supernatural ability* to work through and within us as believers.

First, we're going to examine the ministry of Jesus and how the power of the Holy Spirit operated through His life, as well as His disciples' lives.

> *Luke 3:21 – When all the people were baptized, it came to pass that Jesus was also baptized. And while He prayed, the heavens were opened, and the Holy Spirit descended and bodily formed like a dove upon Him. And the voice came from heaven, which said, You are my beloved Son. In you I am well pleased.*

Jesus had to receive the Holy Spirit before He began His earthly ministry. Until that time, He did not do any miracles. After the Holy Spirit came upon Him, He was immediately led by the Holy Spirit into the wilderness to be tempted by Satan. Once He came out of the wilderness, something powerful happened.

*Luke 4:14 says, "Then Jesus returned in the **power of the Spirit.**"*

That's when Jesus began to **do miraculous things**. He cast out unclean spirits, He healed Peter's sick mother-in-law, and paralytics began to walk. Jesus' ministry was full of stories of healings, deliverances, and miracles.

However, all of these events took place after the Holy Spirit descended upon Jesus during His baptism by John. This marks a pivotal moment. When the Holy Spirit comes upon you, you are infused with power.

Acts 1:8– But you will receive power when the Holy Spirit has come upon you, and you will be my witnesses in Jerusalem and in all Judea and Samaria, and to the ends of the earth.

In Matthew 3:11, John the Baptist said, "There is one who comes after me that is mightier than I, whose sandals I am not worthy to carry. For He will baptize you with the Holy Spirit and with fire."

Jesus is the one who baptizes you with the Holy Spirit and with fire. In Acts, Jesus instructs the disciples in Acts 1, "before you do anything, wait for the promise of My Father," as He understood that they could not effectively demonstrate the kingdom of God in power without the baptism of the Holy Spirit.

In the previous chapter, we explored how the disciples were assembled in one location. It was at that moment

That the powerful, rushing wind of the Spirit surged through the upper room, filling each of them with the Holy Spirit.

Guess what happened next? They went out empowered by the Spirit, glorifying God through preaching, prophesying, and laying hands on individuals for healing, deliverance, and freedom.

Now, let's look at a few verses where the disciples of Jesus begin to actually pray for people to get healed, and delivered, and set free by the power of the Holy Spirit, after the Holy Spirit came upon them.

Your Authority In Christ

The Bible says in Acts 19, verse 11, that "God worked unusual miracles by the hands of Paul, so that even handkerchiefs or aprons were brought from his body to the sick, and the disease left them, and evil spirits went out of them."

After people saw this, some started trying to use the name of Jesus to cast out demons. They said, "We command you to leave by the name of Jesus whom Paul preaches." These individuals attempted to imitate Paul's actions, despite not being saved and lacking the power of the Holy Spirit to cast out unclean spirits. Let's take a look at what happened to them as a result:

Acts 19, verse 15, says, "And the evil spirit answered and said, Jesus I know, Paul I know, but who are you?"

Acts 19, verse 15, says, "And the evil spirit answered and said, Jesus I know, Paul I know, but who are you?"

*Verse 16, "Then the man possessed by the evil spirit leaped on them, **overpowered them, and prevailed against them** so that they fled out of that house naked and wounded."*

The Strength of the Church

Now we understand that Jesus declared in Matthew 16:18-19 that the gates of Hell will not overcome **His church**. However, the people referred to in verse 16 were not believers.

Did you notice the evil spirit said, "**Jesus** I know, **Paul** I know, but WHO are you?"

Note that the evil spirit associates Paul with Jesus in terms of power and authority to cast him out. This implies that when you are **in Christ** and identified with Him, evil spirits cannot distinguish between Jesus and you. That's why the evil spirit challenged those men by asking, "Who are you?" This is because the spirit recognized they were not true disciples of Jesus. Remember, your identity is crucial. Everyone who believes in Jesus is saved and identified with Christ.

Theres one more thing I want to point out in verse 16:

Matthew 16:18-19
And I also say to you that you are Peter, and on this

rock I will build My church, and the gates of Hell shall not prevail against it.

When Jesus said these words, "The gates of hell shall not prevail against it."

He was pointing out that no evil, no idol, and no false god will stand against the greatness of His Body - the Church. Jesus was drawing the attention of His disciples to a visible, existing clash between the forces of good and evil. He wanted His disciples to realize that the enemy is very real and extremely dark. But that is not where the true power lies.

The strength to overcome and the power to be victorious has been given to those who believe that Jesus is the Son of God. It started with the revelation given to the apostle Peter.

Matthew 16:13-18 NKJV
When Jesus came into the region of Caesarea Philippi, He asked His disciples, saying, "Who do men say that I, the Son of Man, am?"

So they said, "Some say John the Baptist, some Elijah, and others Jeremiah or one of the prophets." He said to them, "But who do you say that I am?" Simon Peter answered and said, "You are the Christ, the Son of the living God."

Jesus answered and said to him, "Blessed are you, Simon Bar-Jonah, for flesh and blood has not revealed this to you, but My Father who is in heaven. And I also say to you that you are Peter, and __on this rock I will build My church__, and the gates of Hell shall not prevail against it.

The name Peter translates to "rock," which is significant when Jesus states, "upon this rock I will build my church." This means that Peter's understanding of Jesus as the Son of God will serve as the foundation for the establishment of His Church.

This revelation only comes by the Holy Spirit revealing Jesus as the son of God and what He did on the cross! This is the true church, firmly grounded in their faith in Jesus Christ and His finished work on the cross! The true church understands its identity, embraces the New Covenant of grace, and recognizes its authority given by Jesus! This is the authority and confidence that stems from a genuine revelation of Jesus and what He has done for you!

Take note of the verse that follows Jesus' declaration that the gates of hell will not prevail against it.

And I will give you the keys of the kingdom of heaven, and whatever you bind on earth will be bound in heaven, and whatever you loose on earth will be loosed in heaven."

Not only does Jesus state that darkness will not overcome the church, but the following verse also demonstrates that the church possesses the full authority of Jesus to conquer darkness.

These men performed miracles because they were baptized in the Holy Spirit and with power.

1 Corinthians 2:4-5 NKJV
"And my speech and my preaching were not with persuasive words of human wisdom, but in ***demonstration of the Spirit and of power***, *that your faith should not be in the wisdom of men but in the* ***power of God.***"

Here are some scripture examples of the disciples demonstrating the Holy Spirit's power.

- Acts 9: Peter cures Aeneas of paralysis. Peter brings Tabitha (also known as Dorcas) back to life.

- Acts 14 (verses 8-10): Paul heals a crippled man.

- Acts 16 (verses 16-18): Paul expels a spirit of divination.

- Acts 19 (verses 11-12): Paul performs healings for many people.

- Acts 28: Paul heals Publius's father and others.

There are gifts of the Holy Spirit

There is one final aspect I would like to share with you: the gifts of the Holy Spirit as described in 1 Corinthians 12. While the Holy Spirit bestows various gifts, they all function through the Holy Spirit. Each of us receives these spiritual gifts according to His will, with the purpose of uplifting one another.

1 Corinthians 12:7-11 NKJV
*Now to each one the manifestation of the Spirit is given for the common good. To one there is given through the Spirit a **word of wisdom**, to another a **word of knowledge** by means of the same Spirit, to another **faith** by the same Spirit, to another **gifts of healing** by that one Spirit, to another **miraculous powers**, to another **prophecy**, to another **distinguishing between spirits**, to another **speaking in different kinds of tongues**, and to still another the **interpretation of tongues**.*

*All these are the work of one and the same Spirit, and he distributes them to each one, just **as He wills.***

There's an important point to consider when engaging with the gifts of the Holy Spirit. These gifts function according to **His will**, not ours. This means they operate effectively when we are submitted to the leadership and guidance of the Holy Spirit.

Hebrews 2:4
God also bearing witness both with signs and wonders, with various miracles, and **gifts of the Holy Spirit, according to His own will.**

We have seen a few of these gifts in operation in the scriptures referenced above.

Why do we need the power of the Holy Spirit? The main reason is to testify of a living Jesus. It is very Important that we receive the Holy Spirit's power so that we can be witnesses to Jesus' resurrection and confirm that He is indeed alive.

CHAPTER 5

Salvation and the Baptism of the Holy Spirit

What distinguishes our experience of salvation from our experience with the baptism of the Holy Spirit?

Let's go to Acts 19:1-7.

> *And it happened while Apollos was at Corinth, that Paul, having passed through the upper regions, came to Ephesus. And finding some disciples, he said to them, Did you receive the Holy Spirit when you believed?*

Now watch their answer in verse 3.

> *So they said to him, We have not so much as heard that there was a Holy Spirit. And he said to them, Into what baptism were you baptized? So they said, Into John's baptism.*

In this next verse, Paul explains what the baptism of John was for.

> *Verse 4 - Then Paul said, "John indeed baptized with a baptism of repentance, saying to the people that they should believe on Him who would come after him, that is, on Christ Jesus."*

But they had not yet believed in Jesus. They were repenting of their sins, waiting on Jesus. John the Baptist was sent to prepare the way for the Lord, to get their hearts ready and open to receiving Jesus.

Although they had heard about John's baptism, they were not saved. They were just repentant at heart, awaiting the Messiah.

In verse 4-5 Paul realized they had not heard the Good News that Jesus already died on the cross and resurrected for their sins, so he tells them the Good News of Jesus.

Then Paul said, "John indeed baptized with a baptism of repentance, **saying to the people that they should believe on Him** who would come after him, that is, **on Christ Jesus."**

Verse 5 - When they heard this, they were baptized in the name of the Lord Jesus.

The Gift of the Holy Spirit

They just received salvation because they had put their faith in the name of the Lord Jesus. Now they are ready to receive the gift of the Holy Spirit.

Verse 6 - And when Paul had laid hands on them, the Holy Spirit came upon them, and they spoke with tongues and prophesied.

Now notice the significant difference right there.

They got saved because they put their faith in the finished work of Jesus. Then afterwards, Paul laid hands on them, and they were filled with the Holy Spirit, and they began to speak in other tongues. This was the fulfillment of Jesus's promise in Acts 1:8.

Acts 1:8 NKJV
But you shall receive power when the Holy Spirit has come upon you; and you shall be witnesses to Me in Jerusalem, and in all Judea and Samaria, and to the end of the earth."

It is a wonderful thing that the Holy Spirit comes and dwells in you when you receive salvation. You then become a temple of the Holy Spirit, and He seals your spirit, or else we would not be able to profess the name of Jesus. The Word says that it is only by the Spirit of God can we proclaim the name of Jesus (1 Corinthians 12:3).

Praise God, we have the Holy Spirit dwelling on the inside of us. But it's a different thing when the Holy Spirit comes upon you and anoints you with power, and then you begin to speak in other tongues and prophesy.

Let's look at John 7:37-39, where Jesus promised that the Holy Spirit would be poured out later on in Acts 2.

John 7:37-39 NKJV
On the last day, the great day of the feast, Jesus stood and cried out, If anyone thirsts, let him come to me and drink. He who believes in me, as the scripture

has said, out of his heart will flow rivers of living water. But this he spoke concerning the Holy Spirit, whom those believing in him would receive. For the Holy Spirit was not yet given, because Jesus was not yet glorified.

Pay attention to this: *"But this he spoke concerning the Holy Spirit, whom* **those believing in him** *would receive."* Jesus is referring to people who would already be actively believing in Him, indicating that those who are already born again believers, are the ones who would receive the gift of the Holy Spirit. Therefore, the power of the Holy Spirit is for those who already believe in Jesus. We know this because the very first disciples of Jesus were told to wait for the gift of the Holy Spirit in Acts 1. It is evident they were already saved because these disciples were Jesus' closest followers.

We can even see that after Jesus' resurrection, He visited and spoke with the disciples for 40 days, which proves they believed because they were literally eye witnesses of His resurrection from the dead. After appearing to them, Jesus instructed them to wait for the promise of the Father, the gift the Holy Spirit. The baptism of the Holy Spirit therefore, is a gift from the Father to those who are believers. To provide additional context, I've included the scripture below for your understanding.

Acts 1:2-5, 8 NKJV
"until the day in which He was taken up, after He through the Holy Spirit had given commandments to

the apostles whom He had chosen, to whom He also presented Himself alive after His suffering by many infallible proofs, **being seen by them during forty days** and speaking of the things pertaining to the kingdom of God.

And being assembled together with them, He commanded them not to depart from Jerusalem, but to **wait for the Promise of the Father**, "which," He said, "you have heard from Me; for John truly baptized with water, but **you shall be baptized with the Holy Spirit** not many days from now."

You shall receive power when the Holy Spirit has come upon you; and you shall be witnesses to Me in Jerusalem, and in all Judea and Samaria, and to the end of the earth."

God came to save us by sending His only Son, but Jesus desires to empower us with the Holy Spirit to testify of Him and His resurrection by signs, wonders, and miracles, and by demonstrating the power of the Holy Spirit.

Paul demonstrating the power of the Spirit as testimony of Jesus' resurrection.

Now let's look at 1 Corinthians 2:1-5.

And I, brethren, when I came to you, did not come with excellence of speech or of wisdom, declaring to you the testimony of God.

*For I determined to not know anything among you
except Jesus Christ and Him crucified. I was with you
in weakness and in fear and much trembling. And my
speech and my preaching were not with persuasive
words of human wisdom, but in demonstration of the
Spirit and of power, that your faith might not rest in
the wisdom of men, but in the power of God.*

Now we see right there that the Holy Spirit was demonstrated through Paul's ministry so that the people would see that he was not just another preacher, he was not just another religious rabbi, but that he was there to testify of Jesus Christ. They needed a demonstration of the Spirit's power to show that Paul was offering a new and different way of approaching God.

I noticed by reading through Matthew, Mark, Luke, and John that the ministry of Jesus was very powerful. Why? Because He wasn't just another rabbi, He wasn't just another prophet or a teacher, but He was a Son of the Living God—He demonstrated the power of the Holy Spirit after He received the Holy Spirit in the River of Jordan.

He went out in the power of the Holy Spirit, and He began to heal the sick, cast out devils, and raise the dead. Because of that, there was a large following, and He presented to them the good news that the kingdom of heaven was at hand. And they believed in Him because of the signs and wonders and miracles that He demonstrated.

Let's look at the ministry of Paul when he got knocked off the horse and received the baptism of the Holy Spirit.

Paul, formerly known as Saul, was a very powerful Jewish Pharisee who hated the church of Jesus. He was behind the stoning of Stephen. He really came against the church. But in *Acts 9:10-18*, after Paul encountered Jesus on the road and lost his sight, the Lord instructed Ananias to approach him and pray for him to receive back his sight.

Understandably, Ananias argued with God, pointing out that Saul (Paul) had the power to kill him (as if the Lord didn't already know that.). But the Lord said, No, do as I've spoken. So Ananias did.

And laying his hands on him, he said, Brother Saul, (which the Lord changed his name to Paul). Brother Saul, the Lord Jesus, who appeared to you on the road as you came, he has sent me that you may receive your sight, and **be filled with the Holy Spirit**.

And immediately there fell off his eyes something like scales, and he received his sight at once, and he arose and was baptized. Because Ananias had received the Holy Spirit, he was able to operate in power and restore Paul's sight, then pray for him to be filled with the Holy Spirit. Paul went on to perform many miracles and bring many to Christ through his demonstration of the Spirit.

The reason Paul needed to receive the Holy Spirit is the exact same reason why the apostles needed to receive the Holy Spirit in Acts 2, the same reason why Jesus needed to be baptized in the Holy Spirit in the Jordan River. Every time you ever have a ministry that needs to go forth, you need to be baptized in the Holy Spirit and with power so that you can fulfill the work of God through the power and direction of the Holy Spirit.

I have example that highlights the distinction between salvation and baptism in the Holy Spirit, which can be found in *Acts 8:14-17.*

Acts 8:17-18
Now when the apostles who were at Jerusalem heard that Samaria had received the word of God, they sent to them Peter and John, who came down and prayed for them that they might receive the Holy Spirit, for he had not yet fallen on any of them, but they had only been baptized the name of the Lord Jesus.

We notice here that the Samaritans had already received the word of God, which is the message about Jesus and Him crucified. Immediately, the apostles sent Peter and John to them to impart the Holy Spirit.

During salvation, you don't pray for people to receive the Holy Spirit. Instead, you encourage people to turn their eyes upon Jesus so they can be saved from sin and its wages, death. But afterwards, Peter and John had to come to teach them about and help them receive the Holy Spirit. We can see from this example that receiving the Spirit is different from receiving salvation.

Illustration of the Two Different Experiences

Picture yourself as a glass. Initially, when you are saved, water is poured into the glass, representing the receiving of the Holy Spirit. Now, picture that glass being submerged in a tub of water. This experience is entirely different. Here, the Holy Spirit not only fills you but also envelops you and flows out of you. This is why it is referred to as being "baptized" or immersed in the Spirit.

This is the difference between salvation and the baptism of the Holy Spirit. In salvation, we place our faith in Jesus and His completed work on the cross, resulting in our rebirth through the Holy Spirit. The Holy Spirit enters within us, performing the transformative work of reviving our dead spirits and bringing them to life. At this moment, He resides within us, and we become the temple of the Holy Spirit.

However, when you are baptized in the Holy Spirit, you are empowered, and you begin to speak in other tongues, prophesy, and start functioning in the gifts of the Holy Spirit, as mentioned in 1 Corinthians 12.

The word *empowered* means,
1. Give (someone) the authority or power to do something.
2. Make (someone) stronger, more confident, and effective.

The Spirit of God empowers you, causing you to be strong and filled with God's power, as well as His authority, to be His witnesses with accompanying signs and miracles. He also empowers you to experience a deeper relationship with God and learn more about the mysteries of His nature.

1 Corinthians 2:12
Now we have received not the spirit of the world, but the Spirit who is from God, that we might understand the things freely given us by God.

Both are profound and essential experiences in the life of a disciple of Jesus. Salvation is the foundation of our relationship with God, while the baptism in the Holy Spirit is the divine empowerment that helps us fulfill His mission with joy and purpose. Together, they reflect God's desire not just to save us, but to work through us for His glory.

On the next page I created a comparison chart to help you understand both experiences.

Aspect	Salvation	Baptism of the Holy Spirit
Definition	Being saved from sin and reconciled to God through faith In Jesus Christ.	A spiritual experience where a believer Is empowered by the Holy Spirit for service and witness.
Scriptural Basis	Ephesians 2:8-9 Romans 10:9-10 John 3:16	Acts 1:8 Acts 2:4 Acts 19:1-6 Matthew 3:11
Examples In Scripture	Theif on the cross (Luke 23:39-43); believers In Acts 2.	Pentecost (Acts 2:1-4), Cornelius' household (Acts 10:44-46).
Focus	Redemption, forgiveness of sins, and eternal life.	Empowerment, spiritual gifts, and deeper communion with God.
Timing	Happens at the moment of genuine faith In Jesus.	Upon request (asking the Father in Jesus name) Acts 8:14-17, Luke 11:13, Ephesians 5:18

Aspect	Salvation	Baptism of the Holy Spirit
Primary Role	Restores relationship with God and grants eternal life.	Equips believers for ministry and bold witness.
Manifestation	Inner transformation, peace, joy, and assurance of salvation.	Often accompanied by signs like speaking In tongues, prophecy, or boldness (Acts 2:4; 10:44-46; 19:6).
Requirement	Faith in Jesus Christ alone (Ephesians 2:8-9).	May require prayer, laying on of hands, or seeking God (Luke 11:13, Acts 19:6).
Result	Justification, sanctification, and adoption as a child of God.	Activation of spiritual gifts and greater spiritual sensitivity.
Examples In Scripture	Theif on the cross (Luke 23:39-43); believers In Acts 2.	Pentecost (Acts 2:1-4), Cornelius' household (Acts 10:44-46).

CHAPTER 6

How to Receive the Holy Spirit

Now that we've learned that salvation is different from being filled the Holy Spirit, let's talk about how to be filled with the Holy Spirit. How do you ask? How do you really receive the Holy Spirit?

*Luke chapter 11, verse 9, says "So, I say to you, ask and it **will** be given to you."*

This is not a conditional statement, yet many people overanalyze it. The gospel is straightforward; it's so easy that even a child can grasp it. It's as simple as if somebody wants to give you money, and you just take it.

Only Ask

Jesus is wanting to give you something so much better than money! He wants to freely give you the Holy Spirit to empower you, so that you can be a witness. You only have to ask. The Bible says in Mark 11, verse 24, "Whatsoever things you desire when you pray, **believe that you receive** them."

1 John 5:14-15
This is the confidence that we have in Him, that if we
ask anything according to His will, He hears us. So if
we know that He hears whatever we ask, we know
*that **we have whatever we asked** of Him.*

When you pray, believe that you actually get what you ask for, and you will have it. This is the confidence we need to go into in asking for the Holy Spirit, not because we are confident in ourselves, but we are confident in His word and His promises.

Jesus said, "Seek and you will find" (Matthew 7:7-8).

He also said in the Sermon on the Mount, *"Blessed are those who hunger and thirst for righteousness, for they shall be filled" (Matthew 5).*

Picture yourself stranded in a desert. You've gone two days without water or food, with no signs of either to be found. Could you grasp the intensity of the hunger and thirst you would be feeling?

I'm not sure how you feel, but if I were in that situation, I would search for water everywhere, even the smallest drop of rain. I would do whatever It takes. He says, **ask** and **seek**. Just as you would search for water in a desert, Jesus desires for you to seek Him with that same intensity when it comes to receiving the baptism of the Holy Spirit.

Here's another way to think about it: Imagine someone

tells you there's a stash of gold worth millions sitting on the ocean floor, and they give you the exact location to find it. They point you to the spot where it's hidden.

What you would do? You would get in your boat, and you would go and seek that treasure, because you want to find it. But you would never seek something that was not able to be found. Again, Jesus said, "Seek, and you will find."

If you really want to find what you're looking for, you've got to be super eager—just like a thirsty traveler lost in the desert. You've got to go after it with purpose, knowing that **God wants to fill you** with the Holy Spirit and power. He wouldn't have told us to ask for this if He didn't want us to have it.

Lets look at Luke 11 again. Jesus said, "Seek, and **you will find**." Then He said, "Knock, and it will be open to you." This is just another level of insistence. Knocking is proactive. Do we really have to knock and knock repeatedly? No, because we receive by faith, and we don't have to beg because He *wants to give you* the gift of the Holy Spirit, so we don't necessarily have to be that persistent. But this is about your **hunger level**. We really need to have an eager desire to go after what God wants to give us.

Luke 11:9-13 NKJV
For everyone who asks receives, and he who seeks
finds, and to him who knocks, it will be opened.
If a son asks for bread from any father among you,

will he give him a stone? Or if he asks for a fish, will he give him a serpent instead of a fish? Or if he asks for an egg, will he offer him a scorpion? If you then, being evil, know how to give good gifts to your children, how much more will your Heavenly Father give the Holy Spirit to those who ask him?

Remember, the Holy Spirit is the third person of the Trinity. He should not be viewed as an object, an experience, or merely a power; the Holy Spirit is a PERSON. In a previous chapter titled "The Role of the Holy Spirit," we discovered what Jesus described regarding the Holy Spirit's role in John 14:16.

John 14:16 NKJV
And I will pray the Father, and He will give you another Helper, that He may abide with you forever

I remember when I got filled with the Holy Spirit, I felt a urge in my spirit, and I felt I needed to SPEAK. So I opened my mouth and started to mumble, and the Holy Spirit took over. From that point on, I knew I could pray in tongues all the time.

When the disciples received this promise, they began to speak in tongues as well.

The Holy Spirit comes with supernatural language. However, when you ask to be filled with the Holy Spirit, you must open your mouth and begin to speak as the Spirit of God gives you utterance.

The Bible says in Jude 1:20 - "But you, dear friends, by building yourselves up in your most holy faith and praying in the Holy Spirit."

When we pray in tongues, we engage with the Holy Spirit, enhancing our faith much like recharging a battery. This practice empowers our inner selves, filling us with strength.

I have observed that some individuals receive the Holy Spirit but do not speak in tongues right away, often because their minds interfere. They tend to overthink the experience, doubting whether they have truly received anything, and allowing fear to convince them that they won't speak in "real tongues." This fear often stems from false teachings and the devil's lies, aiming to prevent you from embracing the fullness that God has in store for you.

I have seen many people get filled with the Holy Spirit and speak in tongues. I've prayed for people in Pakistan, Africa, America, India, Ukraine, and all over the world. I've even prayed through the internet, through the phone, and through media, and I've seen people get baptized in the Holy Spirit and speak in tongues immediately. It is such a beautiful thing to see people forever changed.

After you finish reading this chapter, I want you to take a moment and put on worship music, and get very honest with God in your heart. Ask Jesus with all of your heart to baptize you with the Holy Spirit, and you'll feel something stirring on the inside of you. Then open your mouth and speak in tongues. After you do that, we will begin to talk about the deeper things of the Holy Spirit in the coming chapters.

Confidently ask, this belongs to you!

James 1:6-8 NKJV
*But let him ask in faith (**fully confident in receiving**), with no doubting, for he who doubts is like a wave of the sea driven and tossed by the wind. For let not that man suppose that he will <u>receive</u> anything from the Lord; he is a double-minded man, unstable in all his ways.*

The word "receive" in this scripture is the The Greek word **lambano** (λαμβάνω) which means "to take" or "to receive". It can also be translated as "actively receive". So let us not just receive this, but to actually "take" it. The Holy Spirit is not like the devil. He's not going to force you to receive. You have to cooperate with Him. Reach out and eagerly take what belongs to you.

Keep in mind, as you begin to pray in tongues, it doesn't have to sound like something you know. Sometimes it's just a mumble or groan at first. But the Holy Spirit will take over as you begin to speak.

So what are you waiting for? Put down this book and ask for the beautiful gift of the Holy Spirit!

CHAPTER 7

Led by the Holy Spirit

Now that you've received the baptism of the Holy Spirit and your prayer language. Let's talk more about being led by the Holy Spirit. To illustrate this, we'll look at the example of Jesus in Luke 4.

After Jesus was baptized by John in the Jordan River, the Holy Spirit came upon him and he received the Holy Spirit with power.

Luke 4:1-2,14
Then Jesus, being filled with the Holy Spirit, returned from the Jordan and was led by the Spirit into the wilderness, being tempted for forty days by the devil. And in those days He ate nothing, and afterward, when they had ended, He was hungry.

Verse 14, Then Jesus returned in the power of the Spirit to Galilee, and news of Him went out through all the surrounding region.

There is one thing in this verse that I want you to see. The only way that Jesus was able to be led by the Holy Spirit was because first he had to be filled with the Holy Spirit. So it's very vital that we remain filled with the Holy Spirit.

Just as our flesh experiences hunger and requires nourishment to thrive, our spirit also has similar needs. If we neglect to feed ourselves with spiritual sustenance from God, we risk becoming weak and susceptible to the temptations of the flesh. This can lead us to seek the temporary satisfactions the world offers.

God desires for us to live differently. He encourages us to overcome our fleshly desires by embracing life in the Spirit and allowing ourselves to be filled with the Holy Spirit.

The Word of God says in Ephesians 5:18, Do not get drunk with wine, for that is wickedness (corruption), but be filled with the Holy Spirit and constantly guided by Him.

In the context of "be filled with the Spirit," the Greek word for "be" is plērousthe, which means to "be being filled" or "stay in the state of being continuously filled with the Holy Spirit."

It's clear that we need to remain full of the Holy Spirit, but how do we go about doing that? Let's take a look at some scriptural ways we can facilitate this.

After the scripture in Ephesians 5:18, in verses 19-21, it gives us a couple of ways.

Ephesians 5:19-21 NKJV
speaking to one another in psalms and hymns and spiritual songs, singing and making melody in your

*heart to the Lord, giving thanks always for all things
to God the Father in the name of our Lord Jesus
Christ, submitting to one another in the fear of God.*

Another way to stay filled with the Spirit is by immersing yourself in the Word of God and consistently embracing the truth. Did you know that Jesus **IS** the **Word of God** made **flesh**?

*John 1:1 - In the beginning was the Word, and the
Word was with God, and the Word was God.*

Jesus also declared Himself as the way, the **truth**, and the life. The Bible is the Word of God, and it is **truth**. As you continually read and meditate on the Word of God, you are filling yourself with the **truth**. Think about it: in order to be full of God, then we must be full of all that God is — which is **truth** found in His **Word**!

*Jesus said in John 15:7: "If you remain in me and my
words remain in you, ask whatever you wish, and it
will be done for you."*

It is vitally important that we remain in the Word and let the Word of God richly dwell in us as we worship Him, praise Him, and thank Him for who He is and all He has done for us.

Secondly, we can stir up our Spirit by praying in tongues, and by praising and worshiping God. Here are a few examples in the Word of God that show us how to remain full of the Spirit in these ways.

Phillipians 4:6-7
*(this Is to remain **full** of peace): Be anxious for*
*nothing, but in **everything by prayer and***
***supplication**, with thanksgiving, let your requests be*
*made known to God; and the **peace of God, which***
***surpasses all understanding**, will guard your hearts*
and minds through Christ Jesus.

*Jude 1:20 — But you, beloved, **building yourselves up***
*on your most holy faith, **praying in the Holy Spirit**,*
keep yourselves in the love of God, looking for the
mercy of our Lord Jesus Christ unto eternal life.

Praying In Tongues Edifies You

Apostle Paul says in 1 Corinthians 14:18, "I thank my
God that I speak in tongues more than you all."

We can see from this statement that it is to your significant advantage to pray in the Holy Spirit. Praying in tongues Is your personal prayer language to God. When you don't know what to pray, you can pray in tongues.

1 Corinthians 14:2 - For he who speaks in a tongue
does not speak to men but to God, for no one
understands him; however, in the spirit he speaks
mysteries.

One more way continuously remain filled is to surround ourselves with fellow believers and uplift each other in our faith. This creates a profound opportunity to feel His presence and demonstrate His love. Understanding that the Holy Spirit grants us gifts to serve others, engaging in fellowship with other believers is essential for practicing and nurturing the fruits and gifts of the Holy Spirit.

That's one of the primary reasons He was sent: to help us become more like Jesus in our relationships with one another! There's nothing that fortifies your faith quite like sharing testimonies and worshiping together with others. In doing this, we support and uplift one another. All of these things — meditating on the Word, praying in the Spirit, prioritizing time to worship God, fellowshipping with others — have to do with something filling us up.

We need to have something pouring into us daily — reading the Word, listening to worship music, speaking in tongues, meditating on scripture, praying with your friends, or simply getting a piano or a guitar or whatever instrument you can play — or even the instrument of your voice — and just worshiping God, lifting your hands up, and thanking him for what He's done in your life.

All of these things cause us to be sensitive to the Holy Spirit. When we become sensitive to God, we can then be guided effortlessly by His Spirit.

The Word of God says in Acts 6:4, "they gave themselves continually to prayer and the ministry of the Word."

Give yourself fully in your relationship with the Holy

Spirit like you would with a good friend. Put your heart into it, be open, and you'll see exponential growth!

All of the ways I've described here will work. Just start somewhere! As we practice these things through our lives, we are being filled with the Holy Spirit, filled with the Word of God, filled with the knowledge of all the fullness of God, and perpetually creating in ourselves a deeper hunger for God.

Pray and Read the Word to Remain Full of the Spirit

When we remain FULL of the SPIRIT, we are <u>training our ear to hear the Holy Spirit</u>. As we train ourselves to hear the Holy Spirit, <u>He begins to lead us mightily</u>. In my personal experience, I've noticed that during the times I prioritize staying connected with Him and engaging with His Word, I gain significantly more clarity and wisdom in practical aspects of my life. Just like David said in *Psalm 27:4.*

One thing I ask from the Lord, this only do I seek:
that I may dwell in the house of the Lord all the days
of my life, to gaze on the beauty of the Lord and to
seek him in his temple.

David was recognized as a man who truly pursued God's heart. He encountered God's power, wisdom, and strength in various ways throughout his life. Due to his deep connection with God, he understood from personal experience that his hope for leading his people with wisdom completely depended on abiding with the Lord.

Like David, we should aspire to always stay close to the Lord.

David was recognized as a man who truly pursued God's heart. He encountered God's power, wisdom, and strength in various ways throughout his life. Due to his deep connection with God, he understood from personal experience that his hope for leading his people with wisdom completely depended on abiding with the Lord. Like David, we should aspire to always stay close to the Lord.

Remember, How can you follow someone your not looking at? As we put our attention on Jesus, we are able to be led by Him. To truly follow someone, you must actively engage and put your attention on them. This means being present in the moment, listening carefully to what they say. It involves asking questions to deepen your understanding and showing genuine interest in their thoughts and experiences. This same practical approach should be applied when being led by the Spirit.

As you abide in Him, He will begin to lead you. He will give you a strong impression or desire that you will not be able to miss. These impressions and desires will not go away, and that is one way you can know that it's the Holy Spirit. It's important that you tune your ear to be able to recognize His leading.

When the Holy Spirit leads you, He puts a desire in you, and if you don't take action on it, He will remind you throughout your day.

Philippians 2:13
*For God is working in you, **giving you the desire** and the power to do what pleases him.*

Sometimes, you'll just be walking and going about your business. Next thing you know, you'll have this thought that comes into your head about the Word of God or something pertaining to the Lord, or maybe something you need to pray for or do.

You will be able to filter those thoughts, check it with the Lord and say, "Lord, is that you?" Sometimes you'll just know it's the Lord. The Word of God does say that "my sheep know my voice", look at John 10.

*Yet **they will not follow a stranger**, but will flee from him, for **they do not recognize the voice of strangers.**"*

So don't be worried about following the devil's voice, because you are one of His flock. You are his son, you're his daughter. The Bible says in *Romans 8:14, For as many as are led by the Spirit of God, these are sons of God.*

If you're led by the spirit, it's because the Holy Spirit dwells on the inside of you.

The Role of Prayer in Being Led by the Holy Spirit

Oftentimes, prayer is the place where you are led by the Holy Spirit. Prayer is when you're communing with the Lord and you're talking to the Lord.

As you're communicating with the Lord, you might have a particular impression that comes in your mind, a mental image or a flash of maybe a particular song, a person's face, a particular scripture or a particular place you need to go to. You will recognize it because you will see it in your mind, or it will just come up in your spirit, a strong desire to do something.

Maybe you are led to listen to this particular worship song. You might be led to read a book by a pastor or something similar. The Lord leads you in these various ways. There are numerable ways in which the Holy Spirit can lead you. I want to familiarize you with how the Holy Spirit can lead you, because it's important to be able to recognize the leading of the Holy Spirit.

Often, we dismiss these things that the Holy Spirit is leading us to do. We think it's just our own thoughts or fleeting desires. It's very important to pay attention to the voice of the Holy Spirit because he always will lead you into good things.

He will lead you into promotions and jobs. He will lead you to make good business decisions. If there's a business deal in front of you and you don't know what to do, you can always pray and be led by the Holy Spirit either to go forward with the business deal or not. He will even tell you, "There's something not right about this guy," or reveal the other party's motives to you if they're not the right reason. He might tell you, "Just leave it alone."

This is why it's important that you abide in prayer, worship, and feed your spirit. Pour in those good things in your spirit, so that you recognize them when you hear the leading of God.

When you continually practice this, you're tuning your ear to the "frequency" of the Holy Spirit, just like you tune into a radio station. Then you are able to hear Him very effectively.

I want to give another example of how the Holy Spirit leads us in a way we can understand. Say you're just walking down the road one day, minding your own business. All of a sudden, your belly growls, and you're very, very hungry. You have a strong desire after that to get something to eat.

The Holy Spirit and the word always agree

The Holy Spirit is the same way in the way that He leads you. Sometimes you'll just be going about your day, at your job or wherever you are, minding your own business. Suddenly, the Holy Spirit will drop something inside of you. You will abruptly stop focusing on what you're doing and become deeply aware of this particular thing that the Lord has revealed to you, whether it's something about a co-worker, or you need to go home, or you have a strong urge to pray.

When the Holy Spirit leads you or puts a desire on the inside of you, you will always know exactly what you need to do. He gives it that way because God does not lead with confusion. Keep in mind, if it ever feels like confusion then disregard it and have nothing to do with it, and always test everything that you hear by the word of God. The Holy Spirit and the word always agree—just as we talked about in the beginning, that the Holy Spirit is the spirit of truth, and He will lead you into all truth.

Now, actually, in writing this, I am feeling led by the Holy Spirit to share 1 Corinthians, chapter two, with you. That's pretty amazing because we are talking about being led by the Holy Spirit. Let's start with verse nine.

1 Corinthians 2:9-10
But as it is written, eye has not seen nor ear heard
nor have entered into the heart of man the things
which God has prepared for those who love him, but
*God has **revealed them to us through his Spirit.***

You can see that God has the ability to reveal insights to your spirit through His spirit.

1 Corinthians 2:10
For the spirit searches all things. Yes, the deep things
of God.

Do you want the deep things of God to be revealed to you? Would you like the Holy Spirit to guide you into a deeper understanding of the Lord and the immense love of Jesus? Well, He is the one who is able to do that.

Let's continue reading.

1 Corinthians 2:11
For what man knows the things of a man, except the
spirit of the man which is in him.

No one can know your thoughts except for your spirit, because your own spirit is the only one who knows what you're thinking.

1 Corinthians 2:12
Now, we have received not the spirit of the world, but the spirit who is from God, that we might know the things that we have been freely given to us by God.

Notice that it says that *"we might know the things that we have been freely given to us by God."* It is only by the Spirit of God can we say that Jesus is Lord. (1 Corinthians 12:3)

Only by the Spirit of the Lord can we really understand the full revelation of the cross. We see this when Jesus asked Peter, "Who do you say that I am?", and he said, "You're the son of the living God" (Matthew 16:13-20). Jesus replied, "Flesh and blood has not revealed this to you, but the Spirit of the Lord, my Father has revealed this to you."

We can see from that example that the Holy Spirit is the one that reveals the things of the Lord to us and opens up scripture to us.

1 Corinthians 2:13-16
These things we also speak, not in words which man's

wisdom teaches, but which the Holy Spirit teaches, comparing spiritual things with spiritual.

But the natural man does not receive the things of the spirit of God, for they are foolishness to him, nor can he know them because they are spiritually discerned. The person with the Spirit makes judgments about all things, but such a person is not subject to merely human judgments, for "Who has known the mind of the Lord so as to instruct him?" But we have the mind of Christ.

The Holy Spirit Reminds us

The Bible also tells us that the Holy Spirit reminds us of the things that Jesus has taught us in the Scripture.

*John 14:26 NKJV - But the Helper, the Holy Spirit, whom the Father will send in My name, He will teach you all things, and bring to your **remembrance** all things that I said to you.*

He reminds us of things that we've learned, the things he's shown us in the Spirit. He may remind us of a dream that we have forgotten, or reminds us to read a particular verse one day. These are some ways that the Holy Spirit can lead you, not only in your life and practical circumstances, but also into the deep things of God.

I want to remind you that to be effectively guided by the Holy Spirit, we must dedicate time and space to the Lord through prayer and communion with His spirit.

This practice allows us to sharpen our listening skills, enabling us to hear His guidance and voice more clearly.

Remember, being led by the Spirit is a vital part of our walk as a believer. It's important that you be sensitive to the Holy Spirit. If you have a strong desire that keeps continually coming up, and it is in line with the Word of God, don't dismiss it. Give it some thought, give it some prayer, lean into it, and follow the Holy Spirit. This takes action and practice. Don't be hesitant or disobedient, the only way to learn is by taking action.

Listen to His voice. If He's telling you to do something, do it. Don't engage your mind in it and second-guess yourself, thinking, "Oh, that was just me." If it's something He told you that you weren't previously thinking, it's obviously not coming from you. It's from the Holy Spirit. The more you act on His leading, the more you will gain confidence in your ability to hear Him.

When you engage in prayer, be mindful of the guidance of His Spirit. He desires for you to hear His voice because He wants to speak important things to you. It's time to start your journey by listening to the Holy Spirit!

Keep in mind that God is not idly watching from heaven while you navigate life on earth. He is deeply engaged in your journey, eager to lead, guide, direct, and instruct you at every turn, making sure you succeed in all your endeavors. GOD CARES ABOUT YOU! He didn't save you just to let you manage everything by yourself; that's why the Holy Spirit is referred to as your Helper.

*"For I know the plans I have for you,' declares the Lord, '**plans to prosper you** and **not to harm you**, plans to **give you a hope** and **a future**. "* — Jeremiah 29:11.

CHAPTER 8

The Fire of the Holy Spirit

What is the fire of the Holy Spirit? This was a question I asked the Lord many years ago after meditating on Matthew 3:11:

> *I indeed baptize with water unto repentance, but he who is coming after me is mightier than I, whose sandals I am not worthy to carry. He will baptize you with the Holy Spirit **and fire.***

The Holy Spirit led me to concentrate on the next verse, which gave me insight into what this *fire* is.

> Verse 12, *His winnowing fan is in his hand, and he will thoroughly clean out his threshing floor and gather his wheat into the barn, but he will burn up the chaff with unquenchable fire.*

This scripture indicates that the fire represents a separation and consecration. It burns up chaff — waste — and cleans everything up. It separates the good from the bad. It is something that will pull apart, separate, consecrate, and dedicate.

Fire that Refines

Fire refines things to its purest form. Let's take gold, for example. Untreated gold typically has a lot of impure metals in it. What do goldsmiths do? They put the gold in a fire chamber, and they begin to burn it until it becomes completely pure gold, until there is no other metal in it. That's what God does with us. God's refining process is meant to purify and strengthen you, making you more like Him. The Lord is also called "an all-consuming fire" (Hebrews 12:29).

When the fire of God comes on your life, which is also the presence of God, it begins to transform you. It changes you from the inside out. When you yield yourself to the fire of the Holy Spirit, a beautiful process called sanctification can begin. This is a process that goes on throughout your entire life and journey as a Christian.

As we get born again, and and are filled with the Holy Spirit and His power, transformational fire begins to burn within us. The Holy Spirit starts to actively guide our lives, removing people and influences that no longer serve our journey.

Let's take a look at John 15:1-7.

> I am the true vine, and my Father is the vinedresser.
> Everyone branch in me that does not bear fruit he
> takes away, and every branch that does bear fruit he
> prunes, that it may bear more fruit. Already you are
> clean because of the word that I have spoken to you.
> Abide in me, and I in you. As the branch cannot bear
> fruit by itself, unless it abides in the vine, neither can
> you, unless you abide in me.

I am the vine; you are the branches. Whoever abides in me and I in him, he it is that bears much fruit, for apart from me you can do nothing. If anyone does not abide in me he is thrown away like a branch and withers; and the branches are gathered, thrown into the fire, and burned. If you abide in me, and my words abide in you, ask whatever you wish, and it will be done for you.

The reason why Jesus prunes us and removes dead things that produce no fruit In our lives is that He desires you to flourish in your divinely given potential and purpose! When His fire enters your life, illuminating the areas that need to be cleansed and transformed, it allows you see what needs to be changed so you can move more freely and swiftly in fulfilling your purpose.

It is essential to let the Holy Spirit be your gardener, removing the obstacles that hinder your effectiveness and prevent you from bearing fruit. What purpose does a vine serve if it produces no fruit? It becomes worthless. Jesus desires our lives to be vibrant, dynamic, and impactful.

Remember, we are meant to reflect Jesus on this earth; when the world observes us, they should see Him. His desire is for you to mirror Him in every facet of your life, showcasing His strength and power working through you.

Jesus triumphed in every aspect of life and walked with immense authority, fully confident in His relationship with His Father. Because He is victorious, we, as His sons and daughters, are also meant to triumph in every area of our lives. He desires our hearts to be strong and secure in His love while helping us succeed and feel fulfilled while doing the purposes He's put in us.

So remain in the hands of the gardener and embrace change when He says change; allow the fire to burn away what no longer serves you. This serves to demonstrate what a surrendered life to the gardener truly looks like.

Bearing Fruit

In order for a plant to really bloom and blossom to its fullest form, it must be pruned, which means branches that bear no fruit must be removed, so they don't cause the plant to sicken. Then the good branches are free to bear more fruit.

We see in John 15 that Jesus is mainly concerned that we don't lose our **effectiveness** in our life. God's main agenda in the pruning of our branches, the pruning of our fruit — which occurs in the fire of the Holy Spirit — it's to make us more free and His kingdom more effective through our lives. Just like a pruner's shears, the fire of the Holy Spirit consumes everything that is not of God in your life, with the goal that you become a visible reflection of the love and joy and peace of Jesus. This makes us an **effective witness of Jesus** and His kingdom.

Not only do we minister to people through signs, wonders, and miracles and telling about Jesus, but **our lives** also stand as a powerful testimony. They show the transformative power of the Holy Spirit's fire, allowing others to witness Jesus's influence in our lives. It's very important that we yield to this process of the bearing of fruit, yield to the fire of the Holy Spirit, allowing Him to burn everything away that is not of God. Then we can justly show the Father in our lives, glorifying Him through the fruit of the spirit. While the whole world reacts in fear, anger, and unrest, we respond to our lives with faith, peace, patience, and love.

We are able to show the image of Jesus because we have allowed Him to trim our branches, allowed Him to cut things away, to put Himself in us in the place of harmful habits, thoughts, and actions.

This not only produces the benefits of a life lived in righteousness, but also prevents us being caught up in the things of this world. Then we are able to be free from worldly pressures and to really press into knowing Jesus. The end goal of all this is that we may be mature in Christ, shining the light of God to other people, and that we may enjoy the joy of the Lord, the glory of the Lord, the power of the Lord.

Fire Requires Humility

Let's look at 1 Kings 18 where the fire of the Lord came and consumed a sacrifice. This story reveals to us how we must position ourselves to receive the fire of the Lord so we can be transformed.

The false prophets worshiping Baal were taunting Elijah,

telling him that their god was the true god. But Elijah proved them wrong. He did something very powerful. He built an altar and presented a sacrifice.

Verse 36 says, "And it came to pass at the time of the offering and of the evening sacrifice that Elijah, the prophet, came near and said, 'Lord God of Abraham, Isaac and Israel, let it be known that this day that you are God in Israel and I am your servant and that I've done all these things at your word. Hear me, O Lord, hear me, that these people may know that you are the Lord God, that you have turned their hearts back to you again.'"

Then the fire of the Lord literally fell and consumed the burnt sacrifice. You see, the fire cannot come unless there is a sacrifice.

Romans 12:1 AMP
Therefore I urge you, brothers and sisters, by the mercies of God, to present your bodies [dedicating all of yourselves, set apart] as a living sacrifice, holy and well-pleasing to God, which is your rational (logical, intelligent) act of worship.

The word of God says to "present your bodies to God as a living sacrifice." God is not going to override your will and start changing you and molding you if you're not willing. We have to cooperate. We have to yield, which means receiving the Lord, receiving His discipline, receiving the fire of the Holy Spirit. In order to do that, we must submit our lives wholly and completely to God and devote ourselves entirely to Him. Whatever He says goes!

If He says, "Read the Bible for two hours because He wants to spend time with you," you do it no matter what. If He says, "Cut out that friendship that's not bearing any fruit in your life," cut it out. It's very important to listen to the voice of the Lord and allow the fire of the Holy Spirit to sanctify you, to purify you, to tear all those things out, and make His desires your desires.

We want to look like Him, reflect Him, reflect His glory, reflect His love, and be transformed into the image of Jesus. The first thing we need to do is present our bodies as a living sacrifice to the Lord so that the fire of the Holy Spirit has something to consume.

That means presenting all your thoughts, attitudes, opinions, desires, experiences, relationships, choices, weaknesses, and strengths—every part of you and your life—to Him, to do with you what He wants to do. We submit our lives to God and say, "Here I am, Lord—I give You everything. I hold nothing back. If You say this needs to go, it goes. If You say this needs to come into my life, I receive it." When you are positioned like that, the fire of the Holy Spirit and the love of God begin to transform you.

Trust The Process

We don't always know God's reason a for asking us to do

something, but we can be sure it is for out benefit. You will have a testimony of how He loves you, because when He said "cut that friend off," what you didn't know was that friend had intentions to harm you. But God has good intentions for you. He wants to train you and mold you and make you look just like Jesus. He wants to protect you and keep you from harm. At times, we need to let go and trust Him, even when it's hard to understand. When He tells us to move on from a friend, put something aside, or stop watching something, there's always a reason behind it. It is to protect us and bring us closer to Him, because His love for us is so deep.

The reason we give up the things of the world is because they aren't benefiting us anyway. Our true joy in our reborn hearts is to become like Him and to enjoy the benefits of the freedom and the joy of the Lord. The Holy Spirit has to have His way in your life so that He can transform you from the inside out. We can't ride the threshold where we have one foot in the world and one foot in the things of God and expect the fire of the Holy Spirit to begin to change us. We have to present our life completely over to God, submit to God, and walk in His ways.

We must posture out hearts to serve and walk with God and to allow the Holy Spirit to sanctify us. When you're sensitive to Him and His leading and His power in your life, you will get transformed mightily.

During this process of sanctification, joy and the beautiful freedom of walking with Him begins to manifest in your life in visible ways. People are going to say, "How do you have so much joy? How do you have so much freedom?" You will be able to respond, "Because I allowed the fire of the Holy Spirit to transform my life from the inside out. He sanctifies me, He purifies me, and He is faithful." This process is so rewarding because He fills us with so much joy.

Hebrews 12:11 NIV
No discipline seems pleasant at the time, but painful.
Later on, however, it produces a harvest of
righteousness and peace for those who have been
trained by it.

CHAPTER 9

The Holy Spirit, Your Teacher

The Holy Spirit is your *personal* teacher. One of the most beautiful things about that is that the Holy Spirit knows every single thing about you. He's the one who created you. He knows all your thoughts, your emotions, your actions, and He knows what motivates you. He knows how to **teach you in a way that you can understand**. He knows what you like and just what gets your attention. For example, maybe you like science, and He talks to you through science and teaches you about Himself through all the things that you're learning there, even revealing the Word of God through science. Perhaps you like exercise, and He speaks to you through your experience there. He uses anything and everything to reach you.

The Holy Spirit is your friend. It is a beautiful thing to have the very Spirit that raised Jesus from the dead live on the inside of you and lead you and guide you into all truth, knowing He knows everything that you love. So lets explore the various ways in which the Holy Spirit can teach you.

Wisdom and Knowledge

1 Corinthians 2:13
These things we also speak, not in words which man's wisdom teaches, but which the Holy Spirit teaches.

We know that man has a lot of wisdom and knowledge to teach. However, the Holy Spirit's wisdom in teaching us is different. The Holy Spirit has been given to us not only to help us in our weaknesses but also to reveal truth and teach us the Word of God in ways the world could never do.

1 Corinthians 2:10
But God has revealed them to us by His Spirit, for the Spirit searches all things, yes, the deep things of God.

Now, don't you want to understand the deep things of God? Well, the Holy Spirit is the one who has the ability to reveal them to you because He's the one who searches the deep things of God.

Next time you're reading the Word of God, ask the Father for revelation through the Holy Spirit. You can say, "Father, in the name of Jesus, I ask that Your Spirit of wisdom and understanding will completely reveal the Word of God to my heart, that I may know Your Word in revelation, that it might not just be words on a page, that it might be a part of who I am, and that I might be transformed by the Word of God, by Your Holy Spirit teaching me."

The Bible is far more than mere words on a page; however, we can only grasp its true meaning with the guidance of the Holy Spirit.

He Reminds Us

*John 14:26 NIV - But the Advocate, the Holy Spirit, whom the Father will send in my name, will teach you all things and will **remind you of everything I have said to you.***

The Holy Spirit will remind you of things He has taught you. When you allow the Spirit to teach you, you will see the Word of God in such a powerful way that it will transform you. As you're reading, keep your mind open to His nudges, because the Holy Spirit may remind you of another scripture. When He does that, flip to that scripture because the Holy Spirit is trying to teach you. He can do cross-references to unpack the scriptures and reveal the Word of God to you.

It's powerful when you have those times where the Lord, through the Holy Spirit, is giving you revelation upon revelation, bringing you deep into the things of God and revealing those things to you.

The Holy Spirit Teaches Using All Aspects Of Life

The Holy Spirit utilizes all aspects of life to teach us, as He is not confined solely to the Word of God and Christian values.

I also want you to know that the Holy Spirit can teach you the Word of God through the natural things in this world. Jesus taught His disciples not to worry, but to recognize God's nature as a provider by saying, "Look at the birds of the air, look at the trees, look at the lilies of the field" (Matthew 6). He also said, "Look at this fig tree" (Mark 11, Matthew 21). He cursed the fig tree, and then later on, the disciples stumbled upon it. They said, "Jesus, that fig tree that you spoke to the other day is cursed.

Wow, can you teach us how to do that also?" Jesus then used the fig tree to teach them about faith. We see that God uses the things of this earth, like sheep and shepherds, mountains, and all the wonders of nature, to teach us. I want you to be open-minded about the way that the Holy Spirit can teach you.

He can teach you in many different ways. He can use nature, natural situations; relationships, your interests and passions. He can use anything to help you understand the Word of God in its fullness, so it's always good to be open and ready to hear Him speak.

The Spirit of God Will Always Testify To The Truth

I want to talk to you about how the Holy Spirit is the true teacher, as opposed to false teachers. Let's turn to 1 John 2. Here John is talking about false teachers leading you astray, and how the Holy Spirit can teach you to avoid these false teachers.

Verse 26– These things I have written to you concerning those who try to deceive you. But the anointing, which is the Holy Spirit, which you have received from Him, abides in you. And you do not need that anyone teach you, but as the same anointing teaches you concerning all things, and is true, and is not a lie.

No matter what teacher, preacher, prophet, evangelist, or apostle you listen to, always filter their messages through the Word of God, and read it for yourself, and check it with the Holy Spirit. There are many people with many messages and opinions, but the Spirit of the Lord will always testify to the truth.

When someone is teaching with deceptive doctrines and leading the body of Christ astray, the first step is to make sure that what they teach agrees with the Word of God. Also take note that when these false teachers are leading people, we can receive impressions from the Holy Spirit that this person is false. Because you have spent time with the Spirit, you will be sensitive to Him, His thoughts, His ways. You will notice if the message is off, if it's bringing condemnation.

You can always know a false preacher or a teacher by the fruit that they produce. Their messages might bring condemnation, guilt, shame. Romans 8 says, "There is therefore now no condemnation for those who are in Christ." The Holy Spirit always confirms the truth and never supports lies, He is the supreme teacher above all.

It's important to lean on the one true teacher, the one that's been called alongside to help. Let Him help you. Let Him reveal scripture to you, and allow Him to filter all teachings.

He wants to guard you—guard your mind, guard your heart—and make sure that you're walking in a way that is pleasing to the Lord, that is always pointing you to scripture, always guiding you into the truth, and always pointing you to Jesus Christ.

Consider your mind like a little net. No matter what teaching comes through, you have a nice little net that filters lies and truth, and that comes from reading the Word of God and listening to the Holy Spirit. By reading the Bible, you can approve what is the acceptable will of God (Romans 12:2), and you can also detect what is false. The Holy Spirit will help you interpret these truths and remember them.

CHAPTER 10

The Gifts of the Holy Spirit

Before we get into the spiritual gifts, it is essential to understand that, in order to function in these gifts, we MUST be motivated by love towards others. That is where the gifts begin to function.

1 Corinthians 14:1–Pursue love and desire spiritual gifts.

What is the FIRST thing Paul says? "Pursue love." That means as we pursue love, we will begin to desire the gifts of the Holy Spirit, because the gifts serve people and express God's love. Without love, there is no purpose in doing anything, because love is what motivates us to encourage others and build them up.

Think about it. What are the gifts of the Holy Spirit for? To build people up. Why would we want to build up people? Because we love them. Why do we love them? Because Jesus loves them. This is why love must be the center of all that we do.

Look at the ministry of Jesus. What was the reason why Jesus healed the sick, delivered the oppressed, cast out demons? Was it so He could demonstrate the power that He had? No, it was because He loved the people.

Matthew 14:14 KJV
*And Jesus went forth, and saw a great multitude, and was moved with **compassion** toward them, and **he healed** their sick.*

When He saw that they were broken, they needed healing, and they were oppressed by evil spirits, His heart broke for them like a parent's heart does for their child. This is why Jesus came: to destroy the works of the devil.

1 John 3:8 NKJV
For this purpose the Son of God was manifested, that He might destroy the works of the devil.

He could not bear to see His children hurt, broken, and possessed by evil spirits. As a result of His love, power flowed through Him to set them free from the powers of darkness, disease, and death. This is what ultimately led Jesus to the cross to die for us, His love for us.

Paul teaches about the gifts of the Spirit in 1 Corinthians 12, and immediately in the next chapter he states that, without love, everything he just described is meaningless.

1 Corinthians 13:1-10, 13 NKJV
Though I speak with the tongues of men and of
angels, but have not love, I have become sounding
brass or a clanging cymbal.

And though I have the gift of prophecy, and
understand all mysteries and all knowledge, and
though I have all faith, so that I could remove
mountains, but have not love, I am nothing. And
though I bestow all my goods to feed the poor, and
though I give my body to be burned, but have not
love, it profits me nothing.

Love suffers long and is kind; love does not envy;
love does not parade itself, is not puffed up; does not
behave rudely, does not seek its own, is not
provoked, thinks no evil; does not rejoice in iniquity,
but rejoices in the truth; bears all things, believes all
things, hopes all things, endures all things.

Love never fails. But whether there are prophecies,
they will fail; whether there are tongues, they will
cease; whether there is knowledge, it will vanish
away. For we know in part and we prophesy in part.
But when that which is perfect has come, then that
which is in part will be done away.

And now abide faith, hope, love, these three; but the
greatest of these is love.

Now, let's explore these scriptures that reveal the heart of Jesus and the reasons He entrusts us with the power of God.

Matthew 9:35-38, 10:1
Then Jesus went about all the cities and villages,
teaching *in their synagogues,* ***preaching the gospel***
of the kingdom, and ***healing every sickness*** *and*
every disease *among the people.*

Check out the next verse — it shows His heart.

But when He saw the multitudes, He was ***moved***
with compassion for them*, because they were*
weary *and* ***scattered, like sheep having no***
shepherd*. Then he said to his disciples, "The harvest*
is plentiful but the workers are few.

Jesus is moved with **compassion**, and now because there
is a **great need**, He needs **more workers** — that would be
me and you. Watch what occurs immediately in the next
verses:

"Therefore pray the Lord of the harvest to send out
laborers into His harvest." And when He had called
His twelve disciples to Him, ***He gave them power***
over unclean spirits, to cast them out, and to heal all
kinds of sickness and all kinds of disease.

Jesus **gave them power** over these things because they
— and we — are to continue His ministry through the
power of the Holy Spirit.

Now that we understand the motivation of Jesus let's explore operating in the gifts of the Spirit. Keep In mind, our ultimate goal is to edify each other, encourage one another, build each other up, and love one another. It's not about the gift, but the person receiving it. If we have this perspective, the gifts of the Holy Spirit will flow mightily in your life because we'll have the same attitude and mind of Jesus and all the other disciples.

Different Administrations of Gods Power

The gifts of the Holy Spirit mentioned in 1 Corinthians 12 are different administrations of Gods power to heal, do miracles, and edify the body of Christ.

Let's get into the gifts of the Holy Spirit, how they function, how they operate, and how do we receive them. We will go to 1 Corinthians 12 and understand what all the gifts of the Holy Spirit are.

Verse 1 - Now, concerning spiritual gifts, brethren, I do not want you to be ignorant.

Paul's focus in addressing these gifts of the Holy Spirit is to make sure the church isn't unaware of them.

*Verse 4-10 - There are **diversities of gifts**, but the same Spirit. There are **differences of ministries**, but the same the Lord. And there are **diversities of activities**, but is the same God who works all in all.*

But the manifestation of the Spirit is given to each one for the profit in building up of all.

*For to one is given the **word of wisdom** through the Spirit, to another the **word of knowledge** through the same Spirit, to another **faith** by the same Spirit, to another **gifts of healings** by the same Spirit, to another the **working of miracles**, to another **prophecy**, to another **discerning of spirits**, to another **diverse kinds of tongues**, to another the **interpretation of tongues**. But one and the same Spirit works all these things, distributing to each one individually as He wills.*

I want you to notice that the scripture ends by saying the Holy Spirit distributes each gift to each person individually, as He wills. We don't do this ourselves. When we love and serve each other, the Holy Spirit brings forth the necessary gifts for that specific moment.

For instance, if someone is in need of physical healing, you might feel prompted by the Spirit to lay hands on them for healing. This guidance comes from the Holy Spirit, because it's what He wants to do in that moment. The key takeaway is that gifts are given as He desires, especially when our hearts are filled with love and a genuine desire to help one another.

Warning: Remain Inspired by Love

Keep in mind, we must be sensitive to only be inspired by love. The Spirit of God inspires you through love to serve others. The Holy Spirit is God, and God is love.

1 John 4:7-8,11,16 NKJV
Beloved, let us love one another, for love is of God;
and everyone who loves is born of God and knows
God. He who does not love does not know God, for
God is love.

Beloved, if God so loved us, we also ought to love one
another. And we have known and believed the love
*that God has for us. God is love, and **he who abides***
***in love abides in God**, and God in him.*

As long as we walk in love, we never have to worry about misusing the gifts, because that's the whole point in having these gifts: to serve others like Jesus did. The devil can also influence us through wrong motivations, such as self-gain, envy, divination, and witchcraft, by trying to force these gifts. This is a result of our motivation being steered the wrong way by selfish interests or an influence of an evil spirit.

Paul prays in Ephesians 3 that you will be strengthened and empowered by the Holy Spirit, but that you would understand the deep love of God. When you do, **you walk in the fullness of God.**

Ephesians 3:16-19 NKJV
that He would grant you, according to the riches of
His glory, to be strengthened with might through His

*Spirit in the inner man, that Christ may dwell in your
hearts through faith; that you, being rooted and
grounded in love, may be able to comprehend with all
the saints what is the width and length and depth
and height —* **to know the love of Christ which
passes knowledge; that you may be filled with all
the fullness of God.**

We see there that if you want to walk in the fullness of
God, you have to understand the love that Jesus has for
you, so you can **become love.** You cannot release love to
anyone unless you are first receiving love.

Nine Gifts of the Holy Spirit

Before we break down each of the nine gifts of the Holy
Spirit, let's go to *1 Corinthians 14:26*, to understand why
they exist and what they are for.

*Whenever you come together, each of you has a
psalm, has a teaching, has a tongue, has a revelation,
has an interpretation. Let all things be done for
edification.*

The gifts of the Holy Spirit are not for you to use
however you want. They have specific purposes in God's
kingdom. They are intended for building each other up in
love. Every single one of the gifts are going to happen
and flow and function because we want to edify the body
of Christ to reach the fullness of maturity, which is faith

faith in Christ, and to be filled with His love, and to cause the body to work together as a family.

I want to mention that these gifts are available for all believers who are filled with the Holy Spirit and with power, so don't count yourself out on any of these gifts. You can function in any of these gifts because the Spirit of God lives in you, and He is the one who distributes these gifts as He wills.

It is important that you're not ignorant, as Paul said, of these gifts so that you can be receptive when the Holy Spirit wants to perform one of these gifts through you. I will list and describe these nine gifts of the Holy Spirit and their functions according to 1 Corinthians 12:4-10. Let's begin.

The Word of Knowledge

This gift of the Holy Spirit involves having supernatural knowledge about something that you have no ability of knowing based on your human intelligence. I want to share my personal experience with this gift so you can have a frame of reference for some ways it can happen.

Personal Example

While I was at the store doing my shopping, I suddenly felt an inner awareness that someone nearby was experiencing back pain. As I scanned the area, I noticed an individual walking with a cane. I approached this person and offered a prayer for healing, and remarkably, their back was completely restored.

This is one way this particular gift has operated through me. I have also experienced this in another way — by sensing a gentle discomfort in a specific part of my body. It's not painful — rather, it's the Holy Spirit prompting me to be aware of someone nearby who is in pain. In both scenarios, the Holy Spirit gave me knowledge of a condition that required healing so that a gift of healing can be manifested for that individual.

In one instance, I received a word of knowledge about an ankle and noticed a woman nearby who needed healing. I went over to that woman and said, "Hey, would you mind if I prayed for you? I know that God showed me that your ankle was hurting. He wants to heal you." I laid hands on her and said, "In the name of Jesus, I command your ankle to be whole." At that moment, she was completely healed. She ditched the crutches and began to just praise God because she had never experienced healing like that before. It was all because of a word of knowledge — that one word that kept coming to my mind: "Ankle, ankle, ankle." She was so encouraged and felt so loved and seen by God because God knew that her ankle was hurting and wanted to heal her.

The Word of Wisdom

The word of wisdom is a supernatural ability given by the Holy Spirit to provide divine insight, guidance, or solutions to complex situations in the present moment or the future. It is not just human wisdom gained through experience but a direct revelation from God that helps in making right decisions, offering counsel, or discerning the best course of action according to God's will. One of the primary purposes of a word of wisdom is to provide guidance to an individual or a group through supernatural insight into the future.

Practical Examples of the Word of Wisdom in Action

Solving a Difficult Problem

A church leader is facing a conflict between two groups in the congregation. Instead of choosing sides or using personal reasoning, he prays and receives wisdom from God about a solution that brings unity and peace. His decision is something no one had thought of, but it immediately resolves the issue and restores harmony.

Guiding Someone Through a Life Crisis

A woman is struggling with fear about her future, unsure of whether to take a new job or stay where she is. A friend, while praying for her, receives a word of wisdom-an insight that points her toward the right decision, aligning with God's plan. The advice brings her peace, and later, she sees that it was exactly the right choice.

Jesus and the Woman Caught in Adultery (John 8:3-11)

When the Pharisees brought a woman caught in adultery to Jesus, expecting Him to either condemn her or break the law, Jesus responded with divine wisdom: "Let the one who is without sin cast the first stone." This answer not only upheld justice but also extended mercy, leaving the accusers speechless and setting the woman free with a call to repentance.

The Gift of Faith

This gift is a special gift given by the Holy Spirit to allow you to have supernatural confidence.

Whenever you're faced with an impossible situation, an impossible task, or someone that needs to be raised from the dead, something that man cannot possibly accomplish alone, the gift of faith will come upon you. Then you will start to see things the way that God sees things, and God sees no impossibilities, because He formed the earth with a word.

When you supernaturally see how God sees, you will be filled with a confidence that only comes from God, and In this moment, nothing seems Impossible and It gives you the courage to take upon any task that seems Impossible. The gift of faith Is the greatest confidence you could ever feel. It brings you complete certainty and peace. It doesn't even consider circumstances regarding what God wants to accomplish through and with you.

This could be faith for raising the dead, or going for an intimidating job interview, or preaching in front of thousands. You may not even have had any desire to do this thing, but faith bigger than you came upon you, and you got supernatural confidence to go out there with boldness. The gift of faith gives you confidence in God when there Isn't one thread of evidence. It's like standing In the dark but KNOWING the lights are going to come on and God WILL direct your path.

Example of the Gift of Faith

Look at the gift of faith through Abraham in Romans 4:18-22.

> *Who, **contrary** to **hope**, in hope **believed**, so that he became the father of many nations, according to what was spoken, "So shall your descendants be." And not being weak in faith, he did not consider his own body, already dead (since he was about a hundred years old), and the deadness of Sarah's womb. He did not waver at the promise of God through unbelief, but was strengthened in faith, giving glory to God, and being fully convinced that what He had promised He was also able to perform. And therefore "it was accounted to him for righteousness."*

The Gift of Prophecy

The gift of prophecy mentioned in 1 Corinthians 12:10 is one of the spiritual gifts given by the Holy Spirit to believers for the purpose of building up the church. This gift enables a person to speak a message from God by foretelling the future, edifying, encouraging, and strengthening the body of Christ.

I would like to emphasize that we should not mistake this gift of prophecy for functioning in the office of a prophet. The gift of prophecy is not limited to the office of a prophet but is available to all. Look at what Paul states in *1 Corinthians 14:1, to earnestly desire the spiritual gifts, especially that you may prophesy.*

Paul expands on the role of prophecy in 1 Corinthians 14:3, stating that *"the one who prophesies speaks to people for their strengthening, encouraging, and comfort."* This indicates that prophecy in the New Testament mainly involves conveying God's inspired truth relevant to a particular moment, providing wisdom, correction, or insight as inspired by the Holy Spirit.

Unlike the Old Testament prophets, who received direct revelations from God and often foretold future events, the New Testament "gift" of prophecy functions more as Spirit-led communication to guide and edify believers.

Paul emphasizes that prophecy should be tested (1 Corinthians 14:29) to ensure it aligns with God's truth.

There are people who are called false prophets. They can prophesy wrongly to you, and it does not align with what God has spoken to you personally. When someone delivers a prophecy about your life, it's essential to ensure that you resonate with it and that it aligns with truth. If it doesn't, simply disregard it, as many false prophets are emerging in these last days. It's crucial to discern who is genuinely from God and who is not, so take a moment to use discernment when you receive any prophecy.

The Gifts of Healings

The gift of healings mentioned in 1 Corinthians 12:9 refers to a spiritual gift given by the Holy Spirit that enables a person to be a vessel of God's healing power. The phrase "gifts of healings" (plural in Greek) means that this gift can operate in various forms, addressing different types of physical, emotional, or even spiritual healing. This gift functions on an as-needed basis. It's a special ability and anointing that comes upon you by the Holy Spirit to bring God's healing power.

There is a distinction between the gifts of healing and the Great Commission that Jesus entrusted to all believers, as outlined in *Matthew 10:8 — go heal the sick, raise the dead, and cast out evil spirits.* The Bible also says in *Mark 16:17-18, to lay hands on the sick, and they will recover.* However, the gifts of healing operate differently, as they work according to the Spirit's will rather than our own. Let's look at some examples that illustrate the distinction between the two.

Example of the Great Commission at work

Peter was given authority to heal the sick in the name of

108

Jesus. Peter operated In the authority given to him as **He willed.**

Acts 3:6-8 NKJV
Then Peter said, "Silver and gold I do not have, but **what I do have** *I give you: In the name of Jesus Christ of Nazareth, rise up and walk."*

And he took him by the right hand and lifted him up, and immediately his feet and ankle bones received strength. So he, leaping up, stood and walked and entered the temple with them — walking, leaping, and praising God.

Notice that Peter said, "but what **I do have** I give you." What Peter had was the authority Jesus gave him to heal the sick in His name.

Example of the Gifts of Healings at work

Luke 5:17 NKJV
Now it happened on a certain day, as He was teaching, that there were Pharisees and teachers of the law sitting by, who had come out of every town of Galilee, Judea, and Jerusalem. And **the power of the Lord was present to heal them.**

As Jesus was teaching, it is noted that "the power of the Lord was present to heal them." This indicates that, at that specific moment, there was an anointing from the Holy Spirit for healing. This reveals the operation of the gifts of healings, which function according to the will of the Holy Spirit.

My Personal Experience with the Gifts of Healings

During a meeting I was leading, I suddenly felt the powerful anointing of the Holy Spirit rest upon me, focusing on healing. In that moment, I said, "Who is in need of healing? God wants to heal right now." As people began to raise their hands, I prayed for them, and they experienced immediate healing.

The Gift of Working of Miracles

The working of miracles is a creative power that comes upon you from the Holy Spirit to be able to defy nature, defy odds, and do what we call a miracle—something impossible by natural law or human knowledge.

Example Illustrating the Gift of Working of Miracles

I'd like to share an example that illustrates the gift of working of miracles. There was this man who was in Africa preaching the gospel, and suddenly, the gift of working of miracles came on him by the power of the Holy Spirit. He told the crowd, "Bring the dead, bring the lame, bring the people who don't have eyes, bring the people who don't have limbs. God wants to do a miracle."

As they brought those particular people to him, he prayed for them and the dead were raised as the life of God came back into them. They also brought someone who did not have an eyeball or even an eye socket. The eye began to form immediately, and God created a brand new eye, by the supernatural gift of working of miracles. There was also a person who was missing a limb, and it began to grow out supernaturally. It's always amazing when you see the gift of working of miracles in operation.

The Gift of Discerning of Spirits

This gift of the Holy Spirit equips the believer to be aware of evil spirits and that are operating in someone's life. The Holy Spirit pulls back the curtains, exposing the evil spirit, so that the person can experience a breakthrough and freedom from the oppression of the enemy. When this gift is in operation, we can discern whether someone is of the Lord, who's not of the Lord, and also whether there's demonic activity or angelic activity. All of this is discernment of spirits.

This is like the Holy Spirit pulling back the curtains of the spirit realm, allowing us, from the natural standpoint, to see into the supernatural. Maybe that's a sense of knowing, or maybe you physically see a demonic spirit. I've heard people say things like, "I see a snake wrapped around his neck." Is there an actual snake in the natural? No, but in the supernatural, there is a physical representation of a demonic spirit choking the life out of that person. When we sense something like that, we go over and we cast those spirits out and deliver the people. Jesus gave us that command: heal the sick, raise the dead, cast out wicked spirits. He's given us the power and authority to cast these things out. When God gives you insight through the discerning of spirits, as a gift of the

Holy Spirit, take action. He intends to bring deliverance to that individual.

Remember, when God shares something with you, it's not just for your own understanding; it's intended for you to help someone through the guidance of the Holy Spirit.

My Personal Experience

While in a church service, the Holy Spirit gave me the gift of discernment and I began to notice this particular person.

As I looked at her, I perceived a demonic spirit was tormenting her. The Holy Spirit revealed to me that it was a spirit of witchcraft. I could only know that by the gift of discerning of spirits. After the service, I went up to her and cast out the evil spirit.

The Gift of Diverse Kinds of Tongues

The gift of diverse kinds of tongues mentioned in 1 Corinthians 12:10 refers to a supernatural ability given by the Holy Spirit to speak in languages that the speaker has not learned.

Let's look at Acts 2:4-11, where the apostles spoke in an unknown tongue that was understood in various languages by individuals from diverse nations.

And they were all filled with the Holy Spirit and

began to speak with other tongues, as the Spirit gave them utterance.

And there were dwelling in Jerusalem Jews, devout men, from every nation under heaven. And **when this sound occurred,** *the multitude came together, and were confused, because* **everyone heard them speak in his own language.** *Then they were all amazed and marveled, saying to one another, "Look, are not all these who speak Galileans? And how is it that we hear, each in our own language in which we were born?*

*Parthians and Medes and Elamites, those dwelling in Mesopotamia, Judea and Cappadocia, Pontus and Asia, Phrygia and Pamphylia, Egypt and the parts of Libya adjoining Cyrene, visitors from Rome, both Jews and proselytes, Cretans and Arabs — **we hear them speaking in our own tongues the wonderful works of God."***

My Experience With Diverse Tongues

After I finished ministering at a large crusade in Ethiopia, many people approached me for prayer. When three women came forward, I sensed the Holy Spirit stirring within me to speak in tongues, so I began speaking in tongues to them. As I spoke, they started to cry and nod as if they understood what I was saying. (I didn't realize it at the time, but I was exercising the gift of diverse tongues.) Once I finished speaking in tongues, the power of God was so strong upon all of us, including my translator.

Before I prayed for the next group, my translator tapped me on the shoulder and said, "Brother James, Brother James! When did you learn to speak the Sidamo language? While you were speaking, you described every detail of their lives and preached to them!" I explained that I was speaking in tongues under the inspiration of the Holy Spirit and did not know what I was saying. But praise God, they understood me perfectly in their language.

The Interpretation of Tongues

The gift of interpretation of tongues is a spiritual gift given by the Holy Spirit that enables a person to interpret or translate a message spoken in tongues so that others can understand and be edified. This gift works together with the gift of tongues, ensuring that messages spoken in an unknown language are meaningful to the church. The gift of interpretation of tongues is simply the ability by the Holy Spirit to interpret the tongue that was spoken. This can happen whether you are interpreting your own message in tongues or someone else's.

Paul emphasizes in 1 Corinthians 14:5, 27-28 that if someone speaks in tongues publicly in a church setting, there should be an interpreter so that the message can benefit the congregation. Without interpretation, the speaker should remain silent in the church because the message would not be understood.

This can either be for yourself or for the church.

Example

For example, I could be in my home, just praying in the Holy Ghost and speaking in tongues, and I pray, "Lord, give me the interpretation for this." Then, all of a sudden, I'll have a supernatural understanding of exactly what I'm praying for, and that's interpretation.

This can also be an interpretation for whenever you're in a church service or meeting. For example, say someone comes up in church and stands up and begins to speak in tongues. When the Holy Spirit comes upon you and gives you the gift of interpretation, you'll know exactly what that person is saying in order to give God's message to the people.

Learn to Flow with the Holy Spirit

Now that we have explored each of the gifts of the Holy Spirit, we know there are nine in total. Each gift operates through faith, and it's important to remember that the Holy Spirit will not force you to operate in these gifts. He will suggest these gifts to you, but you have to be sensitive to cooperate with Him and allow Him to flow through you. This is what we call yielding to the Holy Spirit. Yielding to the Holy Spirit is just the simple process of feeling an impression from the Holy Spirit — whether it's a word of knowledge, word of wisdom, gift of miracles, gift of faith, gifts of healings, diverse tongues, whatever it is — and not resisting that impression, but yielding.

"Yield" means to give way and allow the Holy Spirit to have His way. If you feel that impression, you have to cooperate with Him by faith. Faith is having the confidence to cooperate with Him and do exactly what the Holy Spirit is leading you to do. The Holy Spirit will guide you and inspire you through one of the gifts. It is essential for you to work together with the Holy Spirit.

He's not just going to do it for you. You can actually resist the Holy Spirit. I know one time I knew I had a word of knowledge for someone. When I saw the other person, I felt scared. I was thinking, "What if this isn't right? It might not work. I'm scared to mess this up." Many times , because of fear, people don't welcome the gifts of the Spirit. Because of my fear in that moment, I did not obey the prompting of the Holy Spirit with the word of knowledge, which was actually going to heal that person if I had done it. But I was afraid. You can suppress the gifts of the Holy Spirit moving through your life, but you will miss out on the blessing of helping someone else and getting to participate in what God is doing.

This is why we need to surrender to the Holy Spirit, allowing Him to work through us. It's important to cooperate with the Holy Spirit, as He desires to accomplish great things in and through us. However, He will not force Himself, as God is loving and respects our free will. He honors us, unlike the devil, who seeks to force his way and manipulate. God does not operate this way.

The Holy Spirit will suggest things to us, bring things to

our remembrance, and reveal things to us. Then we have to actually take initiative with the information that we've been given by the Holy Spirit and put it into action.

When the Holy Spirit gave me that word of knowledge, I should have responded by doing what He was saying. Instead, I missed out on blessing someone and being blessed myself.

Suppose the Holy Spirit is moving in a service, and you get diverse tongues. It takes faith and a lot of confidence to realize this is the Holy Spirit speaking and decide you're going to stand up, give this word in the Spirit, and have confidence that there will be an interpretation. The gift of the Holy Spirit will come upon you, but you have to take action because the Holy Spirit will not override your will.

I mentioned at the beginning of this chapter that every one of these gifts of the Holy Spirit is motivated by love, for edifying people, strengthening them, and encouraging them. It is also important to note that when the Holy Spirit moves through you in a powerful way, do not resist the Holy Spirit because the Holy Spirit wants to move, touch lives, and impact people. The best thing that we can do as believers filled with God's power is to cooperate with Him.

I want to conclude by reiterating this essential statement: it's all about Jesus and His love. It is always, always about loving one another. The Holy Spirit will always glorify Jesus. The gospel is about Jesus — not about us, not about the gifts, not about our works. It's is about revealing Jesus, revealing His love, and releasing that love to other people. When we show the world the deep, powerful, intimate love of God through the power of the Holy Spirit, they will respond to the heart of Jesus — just like the Bible describes in 1 Corinthians 2, that Paul did not come with wise and persuasive words, but with a demonstration of the Spirit's power, because that pointed people to Jesus far more powerfully than a good speech or argument.

I encourage you to pursue love and desire the spiritual gifts because you have the same power of God living on the inside of you that Paul did.

The Bible says in 1 John 4:4, "Greater is He who is in you than He who is in the world."

You have the same Holy Spirit that was in Jesus, Paul, Peter, and John. The same power that raised Jesus from the dead lives inside of you. You lack no spiritual gift. You lack no ability because you have the ability of God in you because the Spirit of God dwells within you. So go out. Start walking with the Holy Spirit. He desires for you to grow in the fullness of God, revealing and reflecting God's limitless power, love, and wisdom to the whole world! God LOVES to take ordinary people and do extraordinary things through them and with them.

CHAPTER 11

Sanctification of the Holy Spirit

As we dive deep in this chapter, it is important to note that the only way to be truly sanctified and transformed is by continuously abiding in the presence of God. When we focus on Him and being in His presence, His presence will begin to sweep over you, causing you to be fully seen, deeply loved, and totally understood.

2 Corinthians 3:18 NKJV
But we all, with unveiled face, beholding as in a mirror the glory of the Lord, are being transformed into the same image from glory to glory, just as by the Spirit of the Lord.

When we abide in this sacred place of sweet fellowship with God, it's almost impossible not to change. Remember, as we discuss walking with the Holy Spirit regarding sanctification, know that God loves you very deeply. He wants you to grow and mature, and this process is called sanctification.

Submitting to the Holy Spirit

When we submit to the guidance and influence of the Holy Spirit, He reminds us of the Word of God and shows us how to make it a reality in our lives. This transformative process not only helps us grow in maturity but also allows us to fully experience the freedom and abundant life Jesus has given us.

We need to recognize that the Holy Spirit desires for us to grow. There is so much to know and learn about God and what we have as His children. The Holy Spirit eagerly desires us to fully embrace everything that Jesus has made available to us as our inheritance. This requires transformation through sanctification, with the wonderful Holy Spirit as our personal guide, helper, instructor, and teacher.

Understanding the Flesh

We are all spirit beings living in a flesh body, this flesh is our fallen nature. The flesh has no positive intentions and consistently steers us away from God's desires. This is what the bible calls the "lust of the flesh." In *1 John 2:16* it says,

> *For all that is in the world — the lust of the flesh, the lust of the eyes, and the pride of life — is not of the Father but is of the world.*

We will have to deal with the flesh as long as we live, however we don't have to do what it desires. Like apostle Paul, we can choose to embrace our new nature and follow the guidance of the Holy Spirit.

In Romans 7:24-25, it's clear that Paul expresses his frustration with his flesh, however he finds freedom in identifying with his new nature.

Romans 7:24-25 NKJV
O unhappy and pitiable and wretched man that I am!
Who will release and deliver me from this body of
death? O thank God! [He will!] through Jesus Christ
our Lord! So then indeed I, of myself with the mind
and spirit, serve the Law of God (God's desires), but
with the flesh the law of sin (sinful desires).

If we don't embrace our new nature, we often will give in to our selfish desires. This is why we must daily submit to the leadership of the Holy Spirit and walk according to our new nature: our reborn spirit. To walk according to this new nature means to *put aside the old sinful nature* and *embrace the new nature* of love, kindness, and righteousness.

Colossians 3:5 AMP
So put to death and deprive of power the evil
longings of your earthly body [with its sensual, self-
centered instincts] immorality, impurity, sinful
passion, evil desire, and greed, which is [a kind of]
idolatry [because it replaces your devotion to God]

Galatians 5:25 also says, since we live by the Spirit,
let us keep in step with the Spirit.

'Living by the Spirit' means fully embracing and

embodying your renewed, born-again identity. 'Keeping in step with the Spirit' means walking in harmony with the Holy Spirit, as He guides us deeper into the fullness of truth.

Our Role In Sanctification

1. Accept your new identity - Understand what the scripture reveals about your identity and what you possess, as well as the significance of Jesus' sacrifice for you, so you can walk In this new way that Jesus has made for us.

Note: It's important to not just hear the teachings from the scriptures, but to also put them into practice in our everyday lives to really experience the benefits and live in the reality of what it teaches.

2. Allow the Holy Spirit to Guide You - Embrace the Holy Spirit's direction in every aspect of your life, allow Him to guide you in all truth. Make sure to fully embrace this guidance in such a way that it fulfills your inner self, leaving no space for selfish desires.

Galatians 5:16-18 NKJV
*I say then: **Walk in the Spirit**, and <u>you will not fulfill the lust of the flesh</u>. For the flesh lusts against the Spirit, and the Spirit against the flesh; and these are contrary to one another, so that you do not do the things that you wish. But if you are **led by the Spirit**, you are not under the law.*

The scripture shows that if you are **actively walking** in the Spirit, you will not satisfy the cravings of the flesh. It doesn't mean that you won't **face temptations** from the flesh; rather, it says that you will not **give in to** (fulfill) those desires.

This is why we need the leadership of the Holy Spirit, because He is the only one who truly knows our needs.

As imperfect stewards of our own lives, we must allow the Spirit of God to navigate our lives due to the corruption and deceptive desires that try to shape us by the darkness surrounding us.

Now is the time for us to let go and allow the Holy Spirit to train us. It requires us to be humble, as the Holy Spirit will lead us toward a path that looks completely different than what the world values. Keep in mind that genuine, lasting transformation requires consistency. We must be intentional about meeting with God daily. Like working out, if you want to see true results and change, it takes consistency over time. Stay true to the journey and remain focused and consistent.

Remember, no one can expect to see results in a single day or even three days. However, with consistent effort over a period of six months to a year, you will notice a significant transformation. So embrace the process and stay committed to the journey, knowing that even if you encounter a setback, you have the strength to come back stronger. God will work with us by guiding us through our challenges.

Since Jesus has liberated us from darkness, we need this sacred training known as "sanctification." It is essential for us to understand how to fully embrace this freedom and adapt to this new way of living.

1 Timothy 4:8 AMP
For physical training is of some value, but godliness
*(**spiritual training**) is useful and of value in*
everything and in every way, for it holds promise for
the present life and also for the life which is to come.

Remember the words of Jesus: "We are in this world, but we are not of it."

John 17:14 (Jesus Speaking) AMP
I have given to them Your word [the message You gave
*Me]; and the world has hated them because they are **not***
***of the world** and do not belong to the world, just as I am*
not of the world and do not belong to it.

This is why we must walk closely with the Holy Spirit because you are going against the very patterns of this world. Just like *Romans 12:2 says.*

Romans 12:2 NKJV
And do not be conformed to this world, but be
transformed by the renewing of your mind, that you
may prove what is that good and acceptable and
perfect will (desire) of God.

Humility Leads to Transformation

As we humbly open ourselves up to change and listen to the guidance of the Holy Spirit, our life will change. We will begin to experience a reality filled with peace, genuine freedom, and love that can only come from having a close relationship with God. As this transformation happens, we will start to see the world through a new lens. This new way of living in the Spirit brings about freedom, love, joy, and peace — qualities that we all crave, even when we might not fully realize it.

Many people seek to fill the emptiness they feel by chasing after things that only satisfy for a moment, thinking that those pursuits will bring them genuine joy and peace.

But here is the issue: these cravings are all driven by **selfish desires**, manifesting as greed, lust, and selfish ambitions. Look at Galatians 5:13-24.

Fruit of the Flesh (Carnal Nature)

Now the works of the flesh are evident, which are: adultery, fornication, uncleanness, lewdness, idolatry, sorcery, hatred, contentions, jealousies, outbursts of wrath, selfish ambitions, dissensions, heresies, envy, murders, drunkenness, revelries, and the like; of which I tell you beforehand, just as I also told you in time past, that those who practice such things will not inherit the kingdom of God.

Fruit of the Spirit (New Nature)

But the fruit of the Spirit is love, joy, peace, long suffering, kindness, goodness, faithfulness, gentleness, self-control. Against such there is no law. And those who are Christ's have crucified the flesh with its passions and desires. If we live in the Spirit, let us also walk in the Spirit. Let us not become conceited, provoking one another, envying one another.

Called to Freedom - Embrace This Reality

Galatians 5:13 NKJV
For you, brethren, have been called to freedom; only do not use freedom as an opportunity for the flesh, but through love serve one another.

You have been liberated from the corruption of this world through the blood of Jesus, and you are now free.

2 Peter 1:3-4 AMP
*For His divine power has bestowed on us [absolutely] everything necessary for [a dynamic spiritual] life and godliness, through true and personal knowledge of Him who called us by His own glory and excellence. For by these He has bestowed on us His precious and magnificent promises [of inexpressible value], so that **by them you may escape from the corruption that is in the world because of immoral desires**, and **become partakers of the divine nature.***

Check out what Paul says in regard to our new nature In Ephesians and Colossians.

*Ephesians 4:20-24 NKJV - if indeed you have heard Him and have been taught by Him, as the truth is in Jesus: that you put off, concerning your former conduct, the old man which grows corrupt according to the deceitful lusts, and be renewed in the spirit of your mind, and that you **put on the new man** which was created according to God, in true righteousness and holiness.*

*Colossians 3:10 AMP - and have **put on the new [spiritual] self** who is being continually renewed in true knowledge in the image of Him who created the new self*

Walk in the Spirit (Your New Nature Given by God)

Galatians 5:16 NKJV
I say then: Walk in the Spirit, and you shall not fulfill the lust of the flesh.

Walking in the Spirit simply means to live in the reality of the Spirit by continually immersing and surrounding yourself with the things of God that build you up, such as godly relationships, worship music, reading and meditating on the Word of God, praying and listening to God, and singing with gratitude in your heart to the Lord.

Remember, God is a **rewarder** of those who diligently seek him. (Hebrews 11:6) The way God rewards you is greater than you could possibly Imagine. Below is just a glimpse of the countless ways in which God rewards us.

- Deep awareness of His power and presence: Seeking God leads to experiencing the Holy Spirit filling us with His presence.

- Inner peace and joy: Being with God can bring a sense of safety and fulfillment.

- Hope and purpose: A relationship with God gives us a source of hope and direction in life.

- Guidance and Wisdom: In challenging situations or when making tough decisions, God can offer us insights and understanding. He provides wisdom to help us discover our purpose and offers guidance along the way.

- Provision and Blessings: God can provide what we need in a single moment through provisions and blessings. He does this by connecting us with others, inspiring innovative ideas, or providing finances in supernatural ways that would normally take years of hard work to achieve.

Ephesians 3:20-21 NKJV
Now to Him who is able to do exceedingly abundantly above all that we ask or think, according to the power that works in us, to Him be glory in the church by Christ Jesus to all generations, forever and ever.
Amen.

As Believers, The Holy Spirit Reveals Righteousness and Not Sin

The Holy Spirit will only convict <u>unbelievers</u> of their sin, because they must recognize their need for a savior. Once they recognize their need for a savior, they repent from their sin and believe in Jesus Christ. At this moment, they become a born again believer.

John 16:8-9 AMP
*And He [the Holy Spirit], when He comes, will convict the world about [the guilt of] **sin [and the need for a Savior]**, and about righteousness, and about judgment: **about sin** [and the true nature of it], **because they do not believe in Me** [and My message];*

Once they are a believer and follow Jesus, the Holy Spirit will no longer reveal their sin. This is because, they have been born again. They have been made holy and righteous. The Holy Spirit will not reveal their sin because they have already been saved from sins dominion and forgiven of their sins.

Ephesians 4:24 NKJV
*and that you put on **the new man** which **was created** according to God, **in true righteousness and holiness.***

Now that you have a new nature and you have a relationship with God, the Holy Spirit will only reveal your new identity in Christ. Jesus no longer remembers your sin, therefore, the Spirit of God will not remind you of your sin, or point out your sin since Jesus removed sin and its effect. Sin has no more power over you and can not remove your right relationship with God.

Isaiah 43:25 NKJV
*"I, only I, am He who **wipes out your transgressions** for My own sake, And I will **not remember your sins.***

Many christians believe if they sin, it separates them from God, or God turns His face away from them. This is false teaching and demonic at its core. By believing this, they are saying sin still has power and God still punishes for sins committed.

We know that the penalty for sin is death. Now, since Jesus took ALL the sin of the world and received ALL the punishment of sin from the Father by dying on the cross. How can God punish the same sin TWICE? It is impossible! Because the principle of double jeopardy states that if a penalty has been paid for a crime, there is no need to make that person pay for the same crime again. Jesus paid for our sins; there is no justice in God making us pay for that sin again.

This is why Apostle Paul writes in *Romans 8:1, "Therefore there is now no condemnation for **those who are in Christ Jesus**.*" So don't beleive the lie that tells you, "if you sin, God Is going to make you pay, or If you sin, God will be disappointed and remove himself from you."

If you believe sin will effect your relationship with God, then you will **constantly walk in fear** of making a mistake, **trying to avoid sin** at every turn.

1 John 4:18 NIV
*There is **no fear in love**. But perfect love drives out fear, because <u>fear has to do with **punishment**</u>. The one who fears is not made perfect in love.*

Instead, realize Jesus set you free and learn who you are and what you have in Christ. Now that you are in the kingdom, it's time to learn what Is in the kingdom and how it operates. Let's get out of focusing on sin and being sin conscious. **Jesus already dealt with sin once for all** so you don't have to walk around being afraid to make a mistake.

Hebrews 10:12-18 NKJV
*But this Man, after He had offered **one sacrifice for sins one for all**, sat down at the right hand of God, from that time waiting till His enemies are made His footstool. For by one offering He has perfected forever those who are being sanctified. But the Holy Spirit also witnesses to us; for after He had said before, "This is the covenant that I will make with them after those days, says the Lord: I will put My laws into their hearts, and in their minds I will write them,"*

*then He adds, "**Their sins and their lawless deeds I will remember no more**." Now **where there is remission of these**, there is **no longer an offering for sin**.*

Jesus wants you to understand the magnitude of what He did for you! You are already free, so stop trying to get free.

Accept what Jesus did for you, thank him, and walk with the Holy Spirit in this new nature God gave you. Jesus has so much to teach you by His Spirit.

So remember, the ministry of the Holy Spirit will always reveal your identity and what you have in Christ once you are a believer. He will not reveal your sin, He will only reveal your righteousness in Christ.

Comparison between Law and Grace

I created a comparison chart to highlight the differences between the two ministries. One represents the law from the old covenant, while the other represents the ministry of righteousness found in the new covenant.

Aspect	Ministry of Death (Condemnation)	Ministry of the Spirit (Righteousness)
Covenant	Old Covenant (Law)	New Covenant (Grace)
Purpose	Reveals sin and brings guilt	Reveals right relationship with God, identity, and inheritance in Christ

Emotional Impact	Produces fear and separation	Produces confidence and intimacy with God
Foundation	Based on human effort and law keeping	Based on God's grace and Christ's finished work

*2 Corinthians 3:9 NKJV - For if **the ministry of condemnation** had glory, the **ministry of righteousness** exceeds much more in glory.*

*Romans 11:6 AMP - But if it is **by grace** [God's unmerited favor], it is **no longer on the basis of works**, otherwise grace is no longer grace [it would not be a gift but a reward for works].*

Change what you value

1 John 3:1 NKJV
Behold what manner of love the Father has bestowed on us, that we should be called children of God!

We no longer should value our works and performances to achieve Gods pleasure and approval of His love for us. We don't have to earn Gods love and approval. Instead, He came to earth through Jesus to show us He loves us, not because we were deserving of love, but because we are His children. He loves us because we are His. That is why Jesus sacrificed His life and was bloodied on the cross for us. He loves us deeply.

You don't have to do anything to show or prove your worth to God in order to receive His love or attention. But rather, **He came to prove and show His love** for us. All we have to do now, is accept and receive His love and walk in companionship with Him.

Just make the Change

During this process of sanctification, its important to know that the Holy Spirit will bring correction and guidance to develop you into who Jesus made you to be. In these times of guidance and correction we don't need to feel shame or condemnation when we make mistakes.

There was a point in my life when I got so distracted from my call. In the moment of distraction, the Holy Spirit reminded me of who I am and how much He loves me. Immediately, I began to cry and tell God how sorry I was. I felt so ashamed and humiliated. Then God spoke to me and said, "Instead of feeling miserable about your mistakes, why not just make the change and feel better? After all, all I want is the best for you." In that moment, I stopped crying and said, "You're right, Lord. What am I doing? Okay, consider the change made, Lord." Instantly, all the guilt, shame, and condemnation lifted off me.

Growth calls for Change

The next time the Holy Spirit leads you away from something, remember to just make the change. There is no shame or condemnation in making changes, because this is how we grow. We have to be moldable In the hands of God. Transformation can be painful as we see In the book of Hebrews.

Hebrews 12:9-11 NKJV
Moreover, we have all had human fathers who disciplined us and we respected them for it. How much more should we submit to the Father of spirits and live! They disciplined us for a little while as they thought best; but God disciplines us for our good, in order that we may share in his holiness.

No discipline seems pleasant at the time, but painful. Later on, however, it produces a harvest of righteousness and peace for those who have been trained by it.

The Ministry Of Righteousness
(The Impact of Focusing on Righteousness)

When you are going off course the Holy Spirit will correct you by revealing who you are and reminding you of the teachings of Jesus. When you remember who you are, you will feel convicted about what you are doing. You will realize it doesn't agree with your identity as a new creation.

The Holy spirit simply reminds us of who we are and how loved we are. These gentle reminders of who we are, speak not to our behavior, but to our HEART. It is only by reminding us of who we are and the love God has for us, can we truly be transformed INTO something.

If you want to see someone change for the better, do not point out their flaws and their shortcomings. Instead, call out their strengths and their identity In Christ.

The Ministry of Condemnation - The Impact of Focusing on Sin

When we point out a persons flaws and shortcomings, you are essentially telling them this is who you are, a failure. What we behold is what we become, and if we are constantly hearing our mistakes, we only continue to fall harder. This is the *Ministry of Condemnation* - the revealing of mistakes.

We know that faith comes by hearing and hearing by the Word of God. We also know that the word 'faith' means to be fully persuaded or confident In something. Well, what do you think happens when we continually remind a person of their mistakes and flaws?

They begin to be fully persuaded that they are a **failure** or **not good enough**. After a while, they will devalue themselves. Because essentially we are building their confidence and faith in their ability to fail and make mistakes. This causes a person to walk around with a guilty conscious and eventually leads to embracing shame instead of freedom.

If we want someone to be confident In who they are and their abilities in Christ, then we must call out their strengths, and reminding them who God created them to be. This is the *Ministry of Righteousness*, the revealing of right relationship with God.

Sanctification through the Guidance of the Holy Spirit

By intentionally seeking God each day, you will begin to notice subtle prompts from the Holy Spirit guiding you in transformation. It is essential to remain sensitive to these gentle nudges or quiet whispers from the Holy Spirit.

These moments of inspiration often happen during quiet times or while praying, nudging you to become more loving, patient, and understanding. Paying attention to these gentle nudges from the Holy Spirit can lead to significant transformation, helping you live more in agreement with Jesus' teachings.

As you go on this journey, you might notice yourself feeling more compassionate and empathetic towards others, wanting to help more, and appreciating the beauty around you. The Holy Spirit's influence can also bring a sense of peace and joy that goes beyond what's happening in your life, helping you stay strong and hopeful even when things get tough.

By remaining **intentional** with your relationship with God, your faith **will grow**, and your **life will reveal** the transformation of Jesus' love and power in your life. Just remember, sanctification is a lifelong journey, a continuous process of learning, adjusting, and developing.

I encourage you to embrace the adventure with the Holy Spirit; it's a transformative experience! So Keep pushing forward and know that you are not alone in this journey.

I'd like to share some of my favorite scriptures that have impacted my life.

1 John 4:13 - *By this we know that **we remain in Him**, and He in us: He has given us of His Spirit.*

Acts 2:17 - *'In the last days, God says, **I will pour out My Spirit on all people**. Your sons and daughters will prophesy, your young men will see visions, your old men will dream dreams.*

1 Corinthians 2:12 - *We have not received the spirit of the world, but the Spirit who is from God, **that we may understand** what God has **freely** given us.*

1 Corinthians 13:13 - *And now these three remain: faith, hope, and love; but the greatest of these is **love**.*

*Romans 5:5 - Now hope does not disappoint, because the **love of God** has been poured out in our hearts **by the Holy Spirit** who was given to us.*

My prayer for you
Ephesians 3:16-20 NKJV

*I pray that He would grant you, according to the riches of His glory, to be strengthened with might through His Spirit in the inner man, that Christ may dwell in your hearts through faith; that you, being rooted and grounded in love, may be able to comprehend with all the saints what is the width and length and depth and height— to **know the love of Christ** which passes knowledge; that you may be filled with **all the fullness of God.***

Now to Him who is able to do exceedingly abundantly above all that we ask or think, according to the power that works in us, to Him be glory in the church by Christ Jesus to all generations, forever and ever. Amen.